Underneath

Underneath

Martin Hayes

Smoke STACK BOOKS

Smokestack Books
1 Lake Terrace, Grewelthorpe, Ripon HG4 3BU e-mail:
info@smokestack-books.co.uk
www.smokestack-books.co.uk

ISBN 9781838465315

Smokestack Books
is represented
by Inpress Ltd

Contents

Some names have been redacted in this work to protect the commercial relationships between certain parties and also to protect the future employment of the writer.

they want all of our teeth to be theirs

they want from us total commitment
they want from us our blood and our hunger
they want our flesh
inked with the company's logo on our chest
they want our knuckles to our brains
and all the nerve-ends in between
switched off
they want our sinews and our muscles
sewn together with steal thread
so that we can only move
when they pull their levers
they want all of our teeth to be theirs
so that we can only chew when they chew
ache when they ache
they want us to show them where we keep our guts
so that they can sneak in under the radar
and pull them apart
angry thread by angry thread
until nothing is held
or stitched together anymore

they want us like robots
sat at our workstations every day
not wanting or able to think
of anything other than what their viruses have burrowed into us
and malfunctioned us to think

and what do we want?

we want to be able to walk through the park on a Saturday
afternoon
without feeling anxious
we want to be able to lay out on the grass
drinking ice cold beer
while looking up into the sky

without worrying about office politics
we want to swim in the ocean once a year
and know how we are going to pay for it
we want a mouth full of teeth
that we know we can afford to get fixed
or capped
if ever they should go rotten
we want to be able to enjoy the laughter and song
that comes from having food in the fridge the electricity bill paid
a car taxed and full of diesel
a medicine cabinet full of floss sticks and Sudocrem
paracetamol and hand cream
Bonjela hair bands
Diazepam and Anusol

we want to be able to live in our block
without the threat of being redistributed
hanging like thick drool dripping from a councillor's panting
mouth
because an entrepreneur took him for a £500 dinner
and promised him a place for his kid in the prep school
that will take our council flats' place
alongside the £65-a-month gym business units
and 1.5 million-pound lofts

we want to feel
be able to say to ourselves
that we are human
and not have to give everything of that away
just so we are allowed to work
just so we are allowed
to exist

why not a job

why not a job
to dedicate your life to
why does it always have to be
a man who died on a cross
or who sat under a fig tree
or who was the last messenger
to bring the words of an invisible and unreachable God to us
those words
don't feed us or keep us warm
they don't feed the homeless man or woman
but a job could put a pair of gloves on their hands
a job could put a hat on their head
help stop them from getting cold
why does a job not get sung out for in churches
have drums beaten for
why not a job that pays for the water and food that goes into
the mouths of our families
wouldn't it be better to stand up for our right to have a job
rather than our right to hold a gun in our hands
why not a job
to wave banners about in the air for
to paint stars in the dark sky for
why not a job
that pays for a roof over our heads
feeds electricity and heat into our homes
rather than a bullet into a 'rag-head' neck
why not a job as our right
rather than these Gods they keep rattling their cages for
why can't these jobs be our Gods
our way of earning a living
the religion we would die for
rather than the colours on a flag

5am early-shift tube ride in

who are these men
with sleepy nests for heads
all wearing the same clothes same
looks on their faces
like something deep down inside them
has cracked

who are these men
holding on
without a skip in their step
hearts mustering an if-you-must pump
spilling just enough blood over its edge
to keep their vast network of veins
and bones and muscle
moving

who are these men
with cracks in their glasses
slumped in their seats
hushed spines sinking into the day's mud
crawling out from under Orgreave's car crash
unable to work out if they have survived
or this is that death

who are these men
in the early morning emptiness
of this vacant lot tube
broken up into millions of pieces
carrying buckets plasterer's poles
De Walt bags drills
hard-hats clipped to rucksacks
or else dangling from forearms
they've got no time or energy
to harm

who are these men
speechless now as worms
bright as flamingos
emptied out into luminous orange suits
SKANSKA – KIER GROUP – GALLIFORD –
BALFOUR BEATTY – MACE –
marked plumage of high-vis vests
marching out onto the salt-flats
to eat
honest as a crow on a slag heap
looking for any old protein or fats
to feed their brood's with
to stuff their nests with
to live on

who are these voiceless men
whose people
are they
our people

the night worker

listen
the night is moving in
as Terry the night controller
steps his way along the canal towards work
watching the sky turning from its busy blue to deep lazy black

he doesn't move with the sea as we move to it anymore
he is a night worker
the dark seaweed has wrapped its fingers around his bruised
barnacled legs
and sets him apart
dragging him down in the opposite direction to the rest of us
the pins and needles of his almost-there heart attack
have stitched him into these night-shift patterns of jet-lag
tolerance
as his wife sleeps in the warm woolen wallet of the loneliness he
gives her
breathes it over her every morning as their ships pass
like a condemned pig's snout exiting air one second before it
collapses
and she now she now can get up to her fussy chattering day

it is the love of mountain lions bears the humpback whale
solitary in the deep depths of their detached existence
two Tenerife toothless weeks the prize sizzling in the pan of their
uneaten breakfasts

never mind
never mind though
it's a job!
and there's always the grass and speed and prescription pills
to help fight the night's army of rogue waves
that wash over him as he watches the clock slowly hammering in its
ticks and its tocks
slowly
slowly the ghosts rise out of his mind dripping wet with mischief
crawling down the inside of his back
dueling in amongst the turrets of his vertebrae
swinging on the nerve-ends of his sciatica
playing out their deep and lonely dramas
that he has become the battlefield and protagonist of

tick tock
slowly the clock goes
carving each second of his shift into his own forearm
until the first cutting-torch-flame of the sun cuts a crack in the black
and light begins to swarm
to the sound of the birds' first song
of kettles boiling over
of bread popping up in their toasters
of the rustle of cereal shaken about in a box
of yawns and pick-me-up kisses
all of the things he misses
or which pass him by
outside the fog
anchored to the top
of his night worker head

kneeling

is first learnt in the house
that is made up of drink
that sometimes catches you on the cheek
because you didn't know yet
that you had to kneel

it is next learnt in the schools
where you sit the tests
hoping you luck-out ticking the correct box of 3 options
of the mathematic test the history test
the geography and science tests
no one wants to know what you think
they only want to see if you have understood
how well you need to kneel

kneeling is next learnt at 16
across the desk of the careers option officer
telling you that you haven't got a hope
of becoming anything like an astronaut
or a professional footballer
and need to learn a trade
that will make the sores on your knees
hurt a little bit less

kneeling is next learnt in the job
under the supervisor's heel
getting ground down by his tongue
wanting to rise up and smack him with your fist
only to bow down
and kneel again
because you now have a roof to pay for
an electricity bill
food
lightbulbs
plasters stamps wine socks

kneeling
gets in the blood
it sticks there
like a scar passed on by each cell
from a long-ago forgotten injury
and it takes a whole lot of energy and magic
for any of us to forget that
try
to stand up again

the moray eels

for all the supervisors in the world

they wait
in their caves
tails up against the back wall
secreting the flesh
that has passed through their bodies
through their ugly insides
into little balls of shit
that pile up behind them like trophies

they have no vision
just these radar screens that wrap the black around their
minds
mapping out the array of activity
just outside their little office doors
where the vast expanse of the sea
stretches its humming and buzzing out

this
is where everything happens
where life takes place
where schools build up into their millions
where one humpback whale can be a city for thousands
where crabs march sideways
trying to take a crust home in their claws
and everything else
goes about its business
hoping it'll survive
to do it all over again the next day

if anything should falter though
if anything should trip
or make the wrong decision
the blackness of their radar screens

light up
and the beeps and pulses
shoot across their boss-eyed inward-looking eyes

mistakes are the only things
that get noticed in their world

then suddenly they snap both eyelids up
a needle tanked full of adrenalin stuck in the heart of a
slumbering beast
and they're out
quick and dumb as a tail of lightning
jaws unpeeled and teeth sticking out
going at their target like something sent from a catapult
snapping a head off
sinking their teeth into an underbelly
pulling insides out
displacing an eyeball here a set of genitalia there
and there is a great thrashing about
in which all of the sand rises up
and mixes with the blood
so that it is very difficult to see
exactly what is happening

then when the sand settles again
all that is left
is the calmness left after death
and them
the moray eels
retracting back into their little caves
feeling the adrenaline begin to peak in their veins
content that they've shown the whole office
who the fucking daddy is again

the other way

you have to work
11-hours a day
give up on your dreams
your life
your loves
because they say it's so

you have to set the alarm clock
to 5am every morning
brush your teeth
be clean shaven
wear an ironed shirt
not stink too much of drink
because they say it's so

you have to get on the tube
£3 each way
in amongst the sweating
the phone-tapping
horrific hordes
because they say it's so

it is the only way
to pay your rent
to pay your electricity
to pay for the food
to pay for the wine
to support yourself
because they say it's so

but there is another way

it lives in your guts
it stares at you
when you look in the mirror

and it hurts
more than anything

it hurts
like a tugboat tied around your waist
like a locomotive
hooked into your eyes

it pulls you towards pain
it pulls you towards less

it pulls you

it pulls you

and the pain is
in the pulling

the not knowing why

if you have it
when you are topping up your Oyster card
you will not understand why

if you have it
when you are in the tube system
trying to get home amongst the hordes
you will not understand why

if you have it
the pain will not be enough to stop you turning up for work
each day
but enough to stop you believing in anything
and you will not understand why

you will seek loneliness
and you will not understand why

you will prefer storms rather than sunshine
sleep rather than wakefulness
darkness rather than light
and you will not understand why

but if your soul
has it in it
if you
have it in you
it is the only way
you can go

and you will not understand why

the weakling

a controller drinks his morning coffee
five shots
he wants to get ready to go in
like Spartacus got ready to leave Sicily
and move in on Rome

he wants to snuff the weakling out of him
stick a full shot of adrenaline in
get his mind ringing
steady and focused
like a sniper's

a controller needs a lot of coffee
scooting about inside him
a half of a Diazepam
a belly full of last night's wine
anything to shut that weakling inside him up

the weakling lives inside all of us
like rust
like tears
like a damaged figurine inside a musical box
like the broken wing
of a little bird
left on the pavement
after a storm

the trees
keep on growing
the frogs
keep on croaking
the whales
keep on singing
but a controller
needs something else

he needs the great writers
the great songs
all swirling about inside him
they tell him that the weakling inside him
needs to be killed

it is hard enough
to do this on your own
sometimes
you have to admit
you need a little bit of help
to get your body over the line
to keep your mind intact
to keep your eyes bright
your heart
pumping
with something else
other than that weakling's fear

the weakling lives inside all of us
it rises and screams for attention
it sometimes makes it impossible
to smile
to survive
to reconnect with your guts

you will not kill it for ever
but you have to find a way
to do it

kill it!

kill it!

and keep on killing it
so that it doesn't feel comfortable
in there

then one day
if you fight well
if you are tough enough
it will leave you
alone

the people who do just enough

we work too much
we love too much
we hate too much
we do everything
too much

we pity too much
we eat too much
we cry too much
and we
moan too much

but the sadness of it all
is we don't do enough

we don't stand up enough
we don't scream enough
we don't set fire to things enough
we rage in our bathtubs and under our showers
we rage from behind our computer screens
we rage at our lovers at our children
at the tv
the radio
the walls
but we don't rage at the correct people
in the right places
in the open air
enough

maybe the poets
who only have £2,000 of their grant money left
and two more applications pending
so that they can carry on writing
about more still life
is just enough

maybe the actors and actresses
who entertain us on the screen
is just enough

maybe the social media avatars
the aggressive personal marketing
the pictures of dinners and cocktails
holidays and selfies
is just enough

maybe we can't sit still
and be silent anymore
because stillnes and silence
is just a missed opportunity
to advance our brand

maybe
all of the noise
is just enough

but it's not enough

nothing is enough

until you are bleeding
until you are out of breath
until you are exhausted
until you have found a way
to separate yourself
from all of the people

who do just enough

hearts bigger than the sun

Chaplin had it
Keaton had it
and Laurel and Hardy had it

Lucas has it
as he walks in early for work
with a flask and tupperware box full of sandwiches under his
arm
with 'mornings' and 'alright mates'
spilling out of him like birdsong
before he sits down at his workstation
spreading it out across the whole room

Javed has it
as he dances across the control room floor
turning and spinning like he's in his favourite Bollywood
movie
tapping colleagues on the shoulder
before leaning down next to them and peering at them with
bulging eyes
doing that thing with his head
from side to side
while wagging a finger at them
before spinning off again
to make himself a cup of tea

Ashley has it
as she sits at her phone station
every now and then letting that laugh of hers boom out into
the air
dirty and gravely as a dockers
that burrows in through our ears
so that it swims in and around our muscles and our veins and
our stomachs
warming up our entire systems

Antoine has it
as he sits at his workstation
carrying on imaginary conversations with controllers
while it's roaring busy and the phones constantly ringing
about how he thinks us controllers haven't had sex in months
or proper kissed a girl since we were teenagers
things totally unrelated to work
that dissipates all of the pressure
and makes you feel
like you're in a school playground once again
rather than in a control room
trying to protect your job

they are the only things they've got left
that they haven't been able to take away from them yet
that despite their snide comments and threats
the traps they set
for them to fall over
in the 3rd year of a pay freeze
with the purchase of the CEO's shiny new Bentley
sitting outside in the yard
hasn't broken them yet

these hearts of theirs
bigger than the sun
spreading their heat and light out
pulling everyone up by the scruffs of their necks
this magical spirit of theirs
that keeps on pumping keeps on
laughing its magic out
even when everything else around us seems to be falling apart
designed
to try and make us give up

lucky charms

some of the people I work with
have made these spaces where they spend 11-hours a day
protected areas
they have developed elaborate internal defenses
that have convinced them that these spots they sit in
are almost sacred
they use plastic figurines pictures stones and cactus plants
to ward off any bad luck that might try to invade them
as every morning these lucky charms
are unlocked from their lockers
and carried like sacred relics to their owners' workstations
where they will all day look down over them
spreading their good luck into the hearts of these men
who just want to get through another day
another week
to another paycheque
as Lenny places the 2 plastic Buddhas of his on top of his
control box
and breathes in a deep breath
before his shift starts
as Antoine crosses himself and kisses the forehead of the
plastic Jesus his mother gave him
just before she died
as Tommy places down his moonstone and mini cactus on the
shelf above his control box
thinking that the spirits of the desert will now be watching
over him
as Robbie never forgets
to pat or stroke the furry head of the troll his dead sister gave
him on his 7th birthday and Bill
blue-tacks back up the 4 pictures of his grandchildren around
his monitor
as a reminder of why he is still controlling and Lucas
hangs a picture of a man starving in a potato field on his
headphones' hook
as his

we all have things we believe in
to thank
for this job
for this still beating blood
for the lady who makes a home for us to come home to every
night
for the car that fires up when you twist the key the numbers
that give us a much needed tenner on the Thunderball
on the last weekend of the month
for the neighbour who helps you lift the freezer up the stairs
watches over your children when you're late home from work
for the insanity of kindness we are still able to show each other
the wine we are yet to drink
the hot water we bathe in
the wolf unable to find your door yet

we all have things to thank
that we believe in
for no other reason than it feels right
because without them
we would take even more magic away from this world
than already has been

all of this blood going on and on

I used to think that God doesn't exist
that it was a thing made of stone
set in old mouths
that grew in graveyards
over plumb trees
and dreams

I used to think that all of the people who believed in it
were ignorant gargoyles
who wanted to fill their hearts
with even more dust
because they were too frightened
by what running blood does

but now I realise that God does exist
because I see it every day in the smiles of my work colleagues
who come in for work
thankful that they still have a job
that will pay for their rent their council tax their food it
exists in the cleaner's hands that holds the cloth that wipes clean
our desks and sinks
all the while singing out aloud to the Taylor Swift songs playing
on his headphones it
exists in Chantelle's hands who makes origami dragons and cats
in between the calls she takes
from customers complaining that their couriers haven't turned
up yet it
exists in the fingers of Bill
whose wife has just been through open heart surgery
yet still comes in on time every day like he has done for the last
18-years
so that he can keep his job
pumping those fingers of his into that keypad
so that jobs can be allocated to couriers
and the whole world can keep on roaring it

exists in the eyes of 17-year-old Laura from the telephonist pool
who fell in love for the first time last weekend
at a party
and came in to tell all the older harder-nosed telephonists
who had been through more men than had died in the first word
war
what love means
how her heart hasn't stopped ringing out like a church bell since
that
is God and it lives
in Magic Mike
who sits under motorcycles winched up on pulleys all day
sticking his fingers up into their sticky insides
so that he can bring those almost dead machines
back to life it lives
in Marcus the van controller
who comes in every day pumped up like a gladiator on coke
ready to make everything happen
with the magic of his tongue the agility of his mind
and the speed of his fingertips it lives
even in Merve
sat hungover in his chair
processing our overnight and international shipments
with his watery red eyes popping out of his head and his hands
trembling
walking out of that office every night
knowing that he is going home to another drink
and a woman who has loved him for over 30-years
who will let him fall asleep in her arms again that
is the God I am on about
the one that lets
all of this blood keep going on and on
like it was what this Universe
was made for

what angels do

I used to think that angels don't exist
that they were characters made up
to make fairy tales and religion feel more magical
wedge open your heart
so that they could then pour all the shit in

but Dolores changed my mind
because she is an angel
the way she takes the new recruits under her wings
teaching them how to do this how to do that
pulling them aside whenever they've made a mistake
looking them in the eyes
whilst explaining to them what went wrong
when every other supervisor just screams at them
thrusts their fangs into their necks
sucking the life out of them in front of everyone else
like they're the runt of the litter
who's way too small to become anything anyway

Dolores doesn't do that
she will pick them up by the hand and sit with them
going over each step again and again
until the new recruit thinks that they've got it
has the confidence to go out into the real world
and attempt to do it all over again

as Dolores follows them out of her office
brushing a stray piece of cotton from the shoulder of her dress
smiling
already looking around for anyone else who might need her
assistance
because that's what angels do

losing Ebony

Ebony from sales
was sent to Paris last week
to deliver a replacement cable for Sony
for a tennis tournament
so that Hawk-Eye could see if a ball
landed on one side of a line
or the other

usually one of the couriers would've been sent
but it was busy
and we needed all of those couriers out there
picking up and delivering the jobs
that kept dropping down onto our screens like confetti
so the supervisors thought
sending Ebony
was the better option

while she was there
she had three-hours to kill after the delivery
before her Eurostar brought her back
to our drudgery

so she sat on the Champs-Élysées
outside a cafe
drinking rose wine
scooping snails out of their shells up into her mouth
which Pierre
soon to be the love of her life
brought to her

neither of them could define it
there was something in his accent
something in her accent

something in the way his bum
sat in his trousers
like two knuckles of a dinosaur fist

whatever it was
they fell in love
and Ebony only came back
to clear out her desk
and hand in her key fob

last seen
they were both sitting in the dust of a trail of a star
heading towards Morocco
with no clothes on
it works like this sometimes
when you least expect it
it rises up
and changes everything forever

but you've got to be lucky

the hardest thing to do in the world

Ashley has only been in the control room for three days
and she is already spreading her fire out
questioning the decisions the controllers make
asking them why
she is having to put up with a customer on the phone yelling at
her
when you 'Mr Controller' said it would all be okay

Ashley
placing her fire under all of those controllers' chairs
because she'd been taught that way
ever since she could remember
encouraged to ask questions
to always be inquisitive always be ready
to stand up for what your heart tells you feels right
and to never get taken for a mug

Ashley
in charge of that heart and blood of hers
rather than letting it overheat her mind and turn it into a mess
turning it around and shining it back at all of those controllers
asking them to explain their decisions
'because it's me who's gonna have to fucking explain it to 'em,
init'
combing her hair out and putting it up in a bun
calling everyone 'hun' except for those controllers
who'd never met an Ashley before
whose idea of a woman in the courier game
was to be silent and 'repeat after me...'

Ashley
not believing in any of it
siting back in her seat
laughing out that great big docker's laugh of hers
letting them controllers know
that they weren't really that special after all
that she'd seen men like them thousands of times before
full of shit and nowhere to dump it
except in somebody else's hands always somebody else's fault
which nine times out of ten
would usually be a woman's

Ashley
only three days in and already calling the controllers out on their
lies
warming up the hearts of all of those around her
who didn't quite have her fire
who didn't quite care as little or as much
about what people thought about them
who'd wanted to say those same words to those controllers for
years
but who hadn't been taught ever since they could remember
to always ask questions
to never let yourself get treated like a mug
to always stand up
for what your heart tells you feels right
even when it is the hardest thing to do
in the world

spines stronger than the back of the Earth

a telephonist's Mum is in our reception area demanding to
speak to a supervisor
so that she can ask him why
her daughter is in tears
and won't come out of her bedroom

the supervisor appears and asks the Mum what the problem is
to which the Mum asks back the same question
only fiercer

the supervisor eventually explains
that this lady's daughter
has a call count 33% below the rest of her team
and despite the counselling sessions she's been a part of
and the warnings she's received
nothing seemed to be improving
so he felt that there was nothing left for him to do
other than try and put 'a rocket up her arse'
which he did do
the afternoon before
when he came out into the telephonist room and in front of
everyone
called her a lazy good for nothing fucking slob
who was dragging the whole team down

the Mum is enraged by this explanation
and tells the supervisor that he should be ashamed of himself
humiliating her daughter like that
in front of everyone
that if it was such a problem
then he should've pulled her into an office and told her so
professionally
like a man would
before swinging one into the side of that supervisor's head
and storming out

thus proving
once again
that you can easily break the spine
of a 16-grand-a-year 19-year-old telephonist
with gold dust in her eyes and a heart like a trumpet
but that a 56-year-old working mum of three
has a spine stronger than any man's
but especially
a supervisor's

Katie and the relocation of her mind

Katie was a creature of habit
she had chronic OCD hoarding issues
and always had to wear something blue
her desk was decorated with artefacts
and lucky charms
that made her feel calm
and safe enough
to be able to concentrate for up to two hours at a time
without having to constantly rearrange everything within
reach

so when the relocation of the office
from Ladbroke Grove to Whitechapel was announced
something deep down inside her didn't want to leave
and just snapped
or ripped
or frayed
or at least
sheared beyond repair

she had lived in Ladbroke Grove since she was born
and apart from a week in Ibiza
for her 18th birthday
and a few weekends at her aunties caravan in Selsey
she had spent her whole life
within those two-square miles

but the relocation process was unstoppable
and as it got closer
Katie began to get more anxious
uncharacteristically taking a day off here
a day off there
having to suddenly leave early some days
for a doctor's appointment
for a dentist's appointment
or because her nan 'had fallen down the stairs'
and she had now to take her to hospital

when it got to the final week before the move
she stopped coming in altogether
sent her supervisor a text
telling her that she was resigning
as she couldn't face the travel
the displacement of the move
had made her split apart
on the inside
to question whether she could even go out to work
ever again
as who knows
what any future employer might have in store for her
after her having invested so much
only to be let down
by this one

there's supposed to be a place for everyone
but some people just can't fit in
or adjust
too much of the good stuff has been let out
to run wild and free
and just being able to keep yourself together
can be enough

awkward Adrian

Adrian received 2nd place for style and technique
in the U-16 Viennese wall climbing championships
back in 2014
ever since
he's been addicted to rock-climbing
travels every night after work the two-hours it takes
from Whitechapel to Latymer Rd
where the largest and most difficult rock-climbing edifice is

there's something in the way it's only you against the rock he says
chalking up the hands
making sure the 'anchors' are in tight
ascending
ascending
your breath hitting and spreading across the cold rock when
you're 'face climbing'
pinching and gripping your way up
feeling the Earth and your parents getting further away
coming to what looks like an impossible pass
having to 'drop knee' to swing around it
then feeling your body move through the air
escaping gravity
momentum
lonely
light

it helped explain the way
Adrian has always seemed so distant
has always had trouble communicating with his work colleagues
who when asking him a question
he would supply the answer of
but in a completely different way than expected
taking them off on a tangent first
leading them towards what he wanted to show them on the way
an excruciating alternative route
talking in his slow deep monotonous voice
like he was up close to a rock
whispering to it
smiling awkwardly making it even more complicated
not really caring if you understand or not
a faraway swell in his eyes
you wanting to shake him
squeeze the answer out of him
as he led you and the conversation around the rock face
towards a far longer but much more comfortable ascent

one he'd learnt to climb many years before
in Vienna
when he was under 16
trying to climb out of his parent's hands

the intern

the intern brought in to help the HR department
organise the warning letters and counselling session minutes
that they leave in big piles on their desks
not having the time to tidy them away into the staff's files
because they're too busy writing up warning letters
or chairing counselling sessions
eats rice crackers
and cucumber discs for lunch
because she says she can't afford much else
what with her being on a 'travel expenses only' contract
whilst she's trying to get some experience under her belt
packing up her CV with ticks and hits
which Chantelle the mother of three telephonist who's
sharper than the edge of a sword
sucks her teeth up at and tells her across the lunch table
that she's fucking mental
working for just the fare in and back home
and then she asks who pays for that?
where you live?
which the intern explains is complicated
what with all her family living up North
not having enough to sort her out with her own room
so she's sort of in between homes at the moment
but reckons that the next month is sorted
because she's shacked up with a bloke she met at Pride – she's
not stupid
and a month is usually the length of time
before they get fed up with you not paying much rent
swerving everything to do with money
to which Chantelle says back
fuck that for a game of soldiers
but the intern tells her not to worry
because it's only for another 9 months
and then she'll have clocked up
the 2 years minimum experience you need

before you can even apply for an HR job
a proper one
one that actually pays
which will help her clear off some of her debt
how she's looking forward to that
to getting some peace and stability back into her life
some of her self-respect back

just hopes she'll be able to find one
that a company hasn't got an intern doing
on a 'travel expenses only' contract

relentless

Chevelle broke down in tears yesterday
not once twice or three times
but four times

it had been a busy day
the sky opened up at 9
and didn't close again till 6
so lots of couriers didn't bother turning up
or were going slow
or disappearing unannounced
so the pressure of covering all the work
started to build up
every 15-minutes producing ten more jobs that couldn't be
covered
until at around 12 o'clock
the screens were two pages full of uncovered jobs
with new ones dropping in amongst them as well

and the customers were continually on the phones
wanting to know what was going on
which along with three others was Chevelle's job to deal with
and even though we'd informed every one of the delays
due to the weather and its impact on the fleet
they still kept calling in
wanting it now
or else their business was gonna close
wanting it immediately
or else they'd lose a million-pound deal
wanting it within the next 10-minutes
or else the photo shoot would have to be delayed
at the cost of £5,000 an hour

it was relentless

and often
when the screens backed up like that
with a supervisor nipping away at you
telling you to get that phone
answer that
email them back quick
criticising the way you dealt with that
or spoke to them
there didn't seem to be a way out
and I think Chevelle felt that yesterday
something inside her felt lonely and exposed
couldn't fight back or defend anymore
and that's when the tears started to come
the 20-grand-a-year she got for doing this
wasn't a plaster big enough
to stop her blood from escaping
so she poured out a little

and it was only when 7pm came around
when she could walk out of there
that everything began to make
a little bit more sense again

call centre women

the telephonist tells me that when she was younger
her mother once bought her a pair of plastic telephones for her
birthday
how she used to make her sit on one side of the room
as she sat on the other
getting her to phone her up
so they could carry out pretend conversations
pretending to be a customer calling up a shop and ordering
things
how funny she finds that
now that telephonist
wears a plastic headset on her head
earning £9.89 an hour
getting fed calls into her from customers
ordering bikes and vans or complaining
that their couriers haven't turned up yet
knowing that every time one of those calls finishes
the phone system will automatically feed another one into her
so that she has no time to stop
or think
about the sun up in the sky
sitting there for 10-hours a day
having to put her hand up first
to ask her supervisor if she can go for a wee
or make a drink
because the only way to stop
those calls continually being fed into her
is to pull the jack plug of her headset out of her computer
disengaging
is not part of the £9.89 an hour deal
though

and I think about all of the women
in all of the call centres of the world
having to put their hand up first
to ask if they can go for a wee
or make a drink
how even the animals can wee when they want to
disengage
when they want to
how even those animals
can look up into the sky
and find the sun
to think about
it's warmth and brightness
guiding them to water
guiding them onwards
and you have to ask yourself
how did all of these call centre women
become less free
than those animals?

Foxconn suicide watch

for Xu Lizhi

they say there are no factories anymore
that they are all now in China
making Apple products and Beats
or in Bangladesh
stitching together Nike trainers and Champion sweatshirts
but ask Judith
and she'll tell you that they still exist
right bang here in the centre of London
sat on her seat for 10-hours a day
with her headset's jack plug
plugged into her computer
that whenever she pulls it out
a supervisor suddenly materialises next to her
like she has just risen up out of the ground in smoke
asking her why she has disengaged
Judith telling her
that she needs to go for a wee
as she says back 'toilet is for breaks'
which she gets two 10-minute ones of either side of her lunch
but often doesn't take
because she has targets to hit
150 inbound calls a day
for 5 days solid
or else her £9.89 an hour pay
gets reduced to £8.72
as Judith crosses her legs
and holds on to her wees
not wanting to get a black mark
pressed into her forehead
not wanting
to not be able to put a bowl of pasta in front of her child's
mouth
or be able to buy a plant

that she can water and watch grow up into the sky
as the system blocks out the sun
drains her blood away
from the heart she's learnt
has to be made to stay awake has to sometimes
be made to keep
on beating
even when all of the rest of you is so tired
so fed up
that all it wants to do is stand up on a roof
and fall
face first
into eternal sleep

your hours

I came to you looking
for a roof to go over my family's heads
for furnishings
for food money
enough left over
to buy socks medicine some wine

thrilled I'd found a way to make all of that work
you put me on the assembly line
amongst all of the other faces
who wanted the same

slowly you turned me into a machine
fused me to a keyboard and screen
poured more hours into me

I became full up

full up with your hours

until there was nothing left of me
but them

training schedule

I always liked it when a new guy came in who had to be
trained
19 fresh out of college and nothing to do with his engineering
B-Tech
me teaching him about how best you can keep the supervisors
off your back
keep your screen clean of all the hot clients *the screamers*
leave the unimportant ones for when you can pick 'em off
to never let yourself get too distended or stressed
making sure that you kept the couriers on your side
not too much
but enough so that they would do anything for you
explaining to him that they were only out there for the money
that you had to feed them
make sure that they could pay their rent their bills their debt
but still have enough left over at the end of the week
 to feel like men
always showing them the respect they deserved
driving and riding around in the wind and rain like that
how it was an awful job
how us controllers
we had to make it feel like we were all in it together

later taking him in to the women in the call centre
them instantly sizing him up
asking me as I introduced him to each one of them
how big his balls were
that he looked like he had a bigger cock than the one they had
back at home
me telling them to stand down him not to listen to them
that they had spent so many years lonely in the dark
that any fresh meat made them feel free and as excitable
as a pack of lions

taking him back into the control room
so he could sit with me and watch
what it was I was on about
the jobs dropping down on the screen like confetti
you having to scoop them all up
hand each single petal over to a courier
linking and weaving the jobs together
so that everyone went home happy
with enough in their bags
and all of the ground left clear
but to be wary of the supervisors
because they had brought men who'd fathered children and
kept homes going for years
to tears before
that there was no way to fight back
because if everything doesn't go according to plan
if customers get on the phone and scream at them
then they will come out and rip you apart
call you names
try to make you feel like you're an idiot
less than worthless
and all in front of everyone else

then after work
taking him over to the pub across the road
buying him a beer
Ronnie instantly cornering him
asking him if he had anything he believed in apart from
money
if he'd ever contemplated suicide
whether he felt like the world was built
to make us all feel like slaves
or something that we needed to take responsibility for
gripping his wrist at the bar later when he went to leave
reminding him to never get too distended or stressed
that it's all like a great big computer game
only with real people's lives at stake

and that was on his first day

the truth

the trainee's first have to spend a day in HR with The Judge
filling out all of the paperwork
signing all of the forms
understanding the company's Health and Safety policy
the company's policy on internet use
the company's policy on sick days and time off
the company's policy on how to lift a box
how you need to bend at the knee
first

then on their second day
The Judge brings them out into the control room
introduces them to that month's designated trainer
so young so unsure
life hasn't burrowed its way into them yet
and begun to destroy them

it is a difficult time
you don't want to scare them off at the first hurdle
but you also can't lie to them
either

so you try to find a middle way
start with the positives
tell them how much this job means to you
how controlling can be such a buzz
sat on the box allocating out the thousands of jobs
all of the couriers out there
relying on you to feed them help them pay their rent
making sure that you give them enough
so that there's enough left over
to make their women love them back
how when it goes right
it can feel like conducting an orchestra
with every single note perfect

how this place
can sometimes feel like the Royal Albert Hall
with you right bang in the centre
of the most beautiful symphony

but you have to caveat that
you have to tell them also
how it can sometimes make you want to crawl under your bed
and not come out for a week
how it can make you turn towards drugs drink
just to mitigate the stress
how they can then easily become your dummy
sucking on them continually
how it can make you sometimes feel unhinged
question everything about humanity
whether a supervisor is of that species
or just an animal who's learned to wear a suit

how it can make you feel rage one minute
then like all of the world is singing together the next

four times I've had it
when they haven't returned back from their first lunch break
The Judge coming out
wanting to know what I'd said to them

the truth
I said back
and nothing but...

growing up

things were looking a little bleak for Kevin
he hadn't been in work for three days
without a call or text
and when he finally walked in
he looked drained
had lost a few pounds
his bones stuck out of his 18-year-old cheeks
like a prisoner's
and his eyes
were a noticeable 8th of an inch
further back inside his head

his supervisor called him over
told him that she and him
we're going in for a meeting
with HR at ten

it wasn't what he'd expected
not what he'd wanted to hear
he wanted to be welcomed back
have an arm put around his shoulder
and asked what had happened
what had gone wrong
why did he look so spooked

but that is what families do
what people who care do
people who Kevin had alienated
with his time keeping
while trying to cross the bridge
over the ravine under where the river runs

the mum whose tv he'd smashed
whose timeframes he couldn't keep
whose constant nipping felt like a flame
placed against his young fuse wire
had given up on him
and the Sunday morning before
when he'd exploded
blown out of orbit
any chance he had of staying
that is when he stormed out

spent three days hanging out on the streets
alone
lonely as a planet in the remotest part of the Universe
with no satellites or moons in sight

hopefully he will only get a warning
will be allowed to resume his position in his telephonist chair
earning £9.89 an hour before tax
so he can at least find a room somewhere
to fold himself up in two of a night

either that
or another one is going to disappear
through the door you've got to keep on
coming and going through
on time
no matter what

Kevin didn't come back

from his HR meeting
he just exited right
out of the door
must've felt desolated
because he left one of his ear pods
and all of his protein drink powder sachets
at his workstation

he'll be out there now
on his own
wondering what to do next
where he goes from here

it is an ugly site
the loneliness
after losing your job
the sky doesn't look so beautiful
the trees don't look so amazing
walking is hard
smiling is hard
breathing
and the hour before bed
not knowing whether you're going to sleep or not
is the hardest

it is the next step
that is always the most terrifying

maybe
I am fussing over nothing
maybe the mum has forgiven him
taken him back in
delaying his final steps
over the bridge
crossing the ravine
under where that river runs

maybe
this poem is pointless
that they are both now sat on the couch
watching family videos together
on the new tele he's bought her
with his last bit of cash

I hope so

magic and sparkle

you should see Bill when he sits down at his controller's desk
he comes alive
like his illuminations have just been switched on
instantly burning away all of the gloom
there's a heat that rises off him that's not there when he's not
controlling
it warms up the entire room
and as he sends those fingers of his down onto that keyboard
he changes
his eyes get bigger
his back gets bigger
he is Eric Cantona with his collar turned up sticking his chest
out to the crowd
he is Michelangelo frantically putting the finishing touches to
his ceiling
Jimi Hendrix holding the meaning to life in his hands
and everyone around him can feel it too
that there is something going on here
they can sense that this man is happy
to be stuck behind his keyboard and monitor
talking to the hundreds of couriers
allocating out the thousands of jobs
in such convoluted patterns
that not even an algorithm has been able to replicate it yet

but I wonder
I wonder if anyone thinks about him on their way home
the way people like Bill
who spread their magic and sparkle out
can change everything make our lives feel better
more illuminated
give us the energy and spirit needed
not to give up
just yet

towards the mountains and stars

Bill has only had cancer twice
which is once less than his wife
who because of her ongoing illness
has had to eBay her motorised scooter
and give up the job it used to take her to
in the solicitors on Watford High Street

Bill hasn't given up his job though
he still gets on his motorbike
with half of his bowel missing
and guns it down the M1
so he can take up his seat at his control desk and work
allocating out jobs to couriers

he still can't find anything else he says
that has even half as much meaning
or gets his adrenaline pumping
as much as this job does
sitting there for 11-hours a day
tapping away at his keypad
watching the couriers on the GPS screen
move around the streets of London

Bill loves it
the knitting and weaving of the jobs together
the subtle intricacies of the allocation process
having to take the couriers abilities into account
the client's expectations into account
the next job coming up the deadlines the earnings
all of it expected by the supervisors to run smoothly
producing no scream-ups no stewards
no account losses

Bill somehow managing to pull it off
making him feel special making him feel connected
walking away after his 11-hour shift
to get on his motorbike and gun it back up the M1
towards the mountains and stars
towards a home where his wife sits in a mask
who he'll hold in his arms and kiss
before replacing her oxygen cylinder
and changing her bag
neither of them knowing how many more shifts
is left in either one of them

the forgotten

the years of ignoring his body
turning all of the alarm bells off
so that he could get in there
and do his job

the years of making sure
that every atom of him
got over the line
wanting and needing to be there
so he could feel connected
not worthless
but a part of something

then when his cells started to give up
couldn't do the time anymore
needed to escape
to rest
go and sit on a park bench somewhere
feeding the ducks
listening to Vivaldi
trying to prolong his life a little
feeding on his memories
and muscle fat

the automatic assumption
from those up in the clouds
was that he was trying to pull a fast one
that he was on the make
cultivating a long-term sickie
that the longest serving controller
the company had ever had
had suddenly gone rogue
was making a meal of it
was maybe forging doctor's certificates
pulling out his own hair
bringing it in to show them
like as if that was actual proof
he had cancer?

as he slipped slowly away
the 15-years of him coming in
allowed to be forgotten
like a note from a trumpet
blown into the air
at a circus

opening up the world

men used to hammer rivets through steel sockets into rock
to secure rails so that trains could
open up the world
the sweat they shed
that wetted the dust
was for their families and the rum they needed to drink
so that they could wear their hearts on their sleeves under a sun
that baked their guts to within one inch of giving up
but they never gave up
they never turned away from that sun
because their families needed to eat and drink
and the world opened up

the men I work with every day
they sweat
they have families that need to eat and drink
they drink rum pop pills smoke snort
they sweat
over keyboards
in front of computer screens where jobs drop down
needing to be allocated to couriers
who risk their lives driving through the streets at ridiculous
speeds
so that the companies who now own those railroads
can open up the world even more

those couriers sweat the same sweat as those railroaders
they grip hold of the handlebars of their bikes
like those railroaders gripped the arms of their hammers
they wear waterproof clothing and balaclavas
like those railroaders wore ponchos and hats
to keep their ears warm
to keep the rain off the skin of their backs
they check the weather on their iPhones every morning
like those railroaders used to look up into the sky they'd just slept
under

hoping it wouldn't make their hearts sink
they spread E45 cream over their crotches
that have become sore and rotten because they have to sit in
puddles of rain
that gather in the seats of their motorbikes
as they drive through the streets
delivering documents that open up the world for the owners of
those railroads
just like those railroaders used to vaseline the cracks in their
hands
from gripping and smashing rivets into the earth with a hammer
all day
opening up the world
for the first time

I guess in the end we are all similar to those railroaders
we all have cracks somewhere
sweat
look up at the sky every morning hoping we don't find it falling
in on us
we all hold our own hammers in our hands
that we want to feed our families with drink rum with open up
the world a little bit more with
so that more than just the owners of those railroads
can get through

dreaming of Lucas

Lucas is the model employee
he is not from the moulds that have cast us
as he walks in 20-minutes early for work every day whistling
old Romanian folk songs
with a smile on his face that has no right to exist
asking everyone in the control room if they want coffee or tea
and we can hear him in there
banging away on the kitchen side like it is the drum of Keith
Moon
waiting for the kettle to heat up
howling out like a wolf along with that kettle
as it begins to boil up like a geyser
coming back in to ask us questions about our evenings and
our women and our children
how he thinks his little 3-year-old might be a witch
because she learnt last night how to spell the word
'immigrant'
with the little wooden lettered tiles that her grandmother sent
over from Romania
as we all sit around dirty with our nights tired and hungover
admiring Lucas for his energy and his verve and his positivity
the way he seems to want this job more than the rest of us
how he seems to be able to absorb the monotony and pain
that years of 11-hour-shifts working in front of computer
screens
can inflict on a man
a man that Lucas hasn't become yet
as he jumps around the control room
never moaning or bitching about the couriers and supervisors
who all pick us up on minor misdemeanors
like it was the end of the world
like we were guilty of murder
as we all sat there petrified of losing these jobs
jobs that paid our rent and our bills enabled us
to walk along a street with our heads held up listen

to pop music drink beers lick ice creams
holiday in Tenerife buy £3 coffees
us for some reason indifferent about them
as Lucas moved his fingertips over his keypad like they were
dragonflies
with a smile always on his face
sending 20% of his wages back to that village in Romania
and that family who didn't have any jobs pulled
potato currency from the dry dusty earth
where that mother of his
still shits in an outside toilet
while looking up at eagles circling the Carpathian Mountains
trying to imagine that face of her granddaughter
hoping that son of hers
hadn't lost any of that famous smile of his
the one the whole village used to talk about since he turned 3
since before he was now
a dream away

well don't worry about that Grandma Lucas
it hasn't been lost yet
that smile of his still exists
it keeps more of us going
than you could ever imagine!

feeling like a man again

some things you can't explain away
like the day Maurice suddenly got up from his seat
and put a keyboard over supervisor Glyn's head
for going one expletive too far
when describing how shit he thought Maurice was
at his controlling job
supervisor Glyn
then running off to the headmaster's office
to head supervisor Harry
to report Maurice for gross misconduct
as Maurice sat there for a moment
letting it all sink in
knowing that he'd finally felt that great big bird arrive
the one he knew was coming
the one he'd sensed was close by
as the sun kept dimming and the skies turned blacker
finally settling in his mind
opening up its 12-foot wingspan
before lifting back its head and
squawking up into the sky
so that it came out of Maurice with him picking up that
keyboard
and smashing it over supervisor Glyn's head
slowly getting up afterwards
picking up his glasses case vape and asthma pump
before silently walking out of that control room
into a bright sky full of sun
its heat
spreading all over his body
finally making him feel
how we should all feel
while still employed in these jobs
that take up a third of our lives
that we are something more than just a pair of hands
who don't need to be spoken to and colluded against

like we are the enemy
who don't need
to be baited and prodded in our traps
until we do something stupid
and have to walk away
unemployed
out into the sun
because all we wanted to do
is feel like a man again

singing like an angel again

Magic Mike made things happen with his fingers and his heart
he rolled those broken bikes tenderly into the workshop like they
were million-pound stallions
with cocks that had gone wrong
and he set about making those bikes' cocks better
by twisting caps and undoing valves
so that he could release the pressure that had been placed on
those machines
winching them up with pulleys onto platforms so that he could
lay under them
and gently put his fingers up into their insides
like an IVF surgeon gently puts his fingers up into a woman's
womb

but Magic Mike only had an engine to bring back to life
which he did by twisting those caps and cleaning pipes that oil
needed to pump through
clean as the blood that runs through a marathon runner's veins
changing parts and calibrating electrics and cleaning down filters
so that those bikes could sing like angels again
rolling them out after he'd finished with them onto the road
outside of that workshop
where he'd hand them back into the hands of 45-year-old biker
men
as tenderly as handing over a piece of newly polished old
jewellery to a lover
men who would now be able to get back on their seats
and gun them through the streets and along motorways
delivering documents and passports as fast as they could
so that at the end of the week they could hopefully earn enough
to put a paycheque into their ladies hands earn a living
that could drop food into their children's mouths
pay the rent the council tax the electricity bill
and still have enough left over to put towards their next tattoo
as Magic Mike disappeared back into the workshop

with his fingers and his heart
to sit on his dirty old chair
listening to trap on his headphones
not knowing or having a clue
about half as much
as he was keeping this world together

back in the game

we often wonder how the new old-hand applicant feels
when he is led into that goldfish bowl of a supervisor's office to
start his interview
how he must feel
having to explain why he is the right man for the job once again
dredge up the details of those 20-years of experience he's had in
control rooms
the reason why he is out of work
how excited he is to be so close to feeling like a man again
so close that only the glass of that office
separates him from the buzz of us employed controllers
the noise and scent of that pack
held back by just 3 millimeters of glass
how he must feel it all begin to stir inside him again
feel his fingers begin to throb a little itching to get at those
keyboards
taste the shifts at the back of his throat the money in his hands
his heart
begin to pump again
waking up that pointless and tired blood of his
feeling almost alive for the very first time
since he was last employed

he must stay calm though

he can't let the supervisor see
that he is desperate to get back into one of them controller's
chairs
desperate to get back in amongst that pack
swapping shifts and telling tall tales about your woman
back driving into work
with the window open the music turned up
smoking down a cigarette and flicking it out into the sky
like a modern-day Marlon Brando
back in the game of buying things
like coffees and beers and ice creams socks and fresh pants
back feeling life fire itself through you once again
where your bare hands can now reach again into the sun
and lift it up over the line
where your woman starts to hold you once again
like she actually means it
and you notice
the birds singing on chimney pots the colour of the trees
the wagging of a dog's tail the stretching of a cat
the way the sun feels
on your back
as you walk along the street
with your head held up
and even the bills and the thunder and rain
feel like they are part of the plan

the souls of men

it's amazing the amount of men who keep coming
through the doors of this control room
wanting to drive these vans of ours
for 10-hours a day
it is like there is a great big reservoir of them
that never dries up
crawling out through the cracks in the bedrock
fighting one another to get to the shore
so that they can arrive here
and walk through these glass doors
to pick up a pair of keys in their hands
and jump into one of our vans

and for what?
to sit in traffic all day?
to get flashed for driving too fast?
to get ticketed for parking on yellow lines and red routes
just so they can deliver their parcels on time?
getting fined
for taking the wrong turn?
for just trying too hard?
so that when it all gets too much
they end up screaming out of the cabins of their vans
words they use
to remind themselves
that they are still just about alive

it's amazing the amount of men who keep coming
through the doors of this control room
wanting to drive these vans of ours
it is like there must be some kind of cauldron somewhere
where the souls of these men
are gently stirred until they are formed enough
to grab onto the tails of smoke rising up into the air
only to let go and float down
to land outside these glass doors of ours
looking for a job

you'd think that some of the returning souls
would have a word with them
give them the heads up
about not going for that van driving job

you'd think they'd let them know
to choose something different
like jumping into the body of a dust mite
clinging to the walls of the next Mozarts' piano
as he writes the next Moonlight Sonata
or seeking out the body of a CEO
whose fingertips only have to worry
about lifting a glass of silky wine to his lips
or tapping the ash from his cigar
into the centre of a crystal ashtray
anything
but that van driving job

but they keep coming
to drive these vans of ours
because for some it is the only way they can earn a living put a
lolly
into their child's mouth
buy a bunch of roses for their lady on Valentine's Day
pay for the electricity that keeps them warm at night
replace the broken tele of their 83-year-old Mum
so she can still watch her David Attenborough programmes
whenever she wants
and not feel like giving up yet

it's how they hang on
to that feeling
that they mean something
that despite everything
they are at least going to try to find a way
that enables them to walk through the fire
with their heads up
before their soul's finally give up trying
and head back to that reservoir
once again

we need payslips

we work to make it turn into food
to make it turn into heat and electricity that keeps our families
warm and happy we work
for the council tax the rent the laughter and song
we work like Standing Bear worked we all work
for the hill in the mists at the back of our minds that we were
brought up on
the land where we once ran free
alongside our buffalo alongside our canal our dogs
the city rat knows this
and the turtle in the sea knows it
we all work to make our skirting-board Empires happen
as Elon Musk colonises space and all the stars are bought
by money

while our Empires
spread themselves out to just the next Saturday afternoon
sat outside pubs in parks drinking up the sun
waving a payslip about in our hands with laughter in our
throats
a payslip that will pay for the ice creams the cake the coffees
the beers and wine that make it all just about bearable
a payslip that wherever you are
stretches the whole route back to work
building you making you the strength of rivets that hold
together ships
that won't fall apart in the middle of the ocean
payslips that are the jaws of a leopard
that can drag its prey up into a tree and eat peacefully for a
week
payslips made by hours spent tapping away at buttons
ignoring the snide comments of supervisors
turning our cheeks and dignity towards the sun
and what those payslips will bring us
payslips that make things happen
payslips that keep our hearts intact and stuck together

fuck the dignity of labour
we need payslips
we need food and wine on the table
we need heat in the water that comes out of our taps
we need cigarettes to smoke internet connections floss sticks
toothpaste E45 and hair clips
we need washing up liquid hoover-bags and batteries
we need light bulbs socks and scissors to cut the gaffer tape
that keep our remote controls together
we need beds
beds we can fuck in beds we can sleep in
beds we can sweat in and beds we can die in
we need
TO EXIST!
under a roof
that only our payslips can provide

they keep us so busy

put that piece of paper here
that piece of paper there
carry that folder up the stairs
carry that report down the stairs
answer this phone
answer that phone
move those boxes from this corner of the warehouse
to that corner of the warehouse
then back again

it is exhausting

on the tube
they make us herd in
pressed up against each other
our shins and eyelashes
our ear-hairs and arseholes
all inches away from each other's groins
stuck in the faces of those lucky enough to get seats
delayed in tunnels
a quarter of a mile under the Earth
because someone couldn't take it anymore
and threw themselves on the tracks

and when we get there
we pour out slipping in behind each other
single file slow moving up the stairs
arseholes in our faces
reminding us of the animals we are considered
sniffing each other's cracks amongst the disease and shit
before we escalate ourselves back out
into the light and air

it is exhausting

they keep us so busy
pumping away at keypads
documenting numbers
filling in forms and time sheets
answering phones
learning systems and procedures
learning their language
'going forwards'
'let's take this offline'
'high levels of churn'
'the root of the problem'
language made up in their clouds
where Zeus and Hera now sit
pouring over spreadsheets
instead of chessboards

and there are clocks everywhere
on the walls
in the corners of our monitors
digital ones analogue ones
clocks that slowly go tick
clocks that click clocks that flip
clocks even in the toilets

and then after 11-hours of that
it's back in on the tube home
back in with the shins and eyelashes
the ear-hairs and arseholes

they keep us so busy

it is exhausting

sometimes it's all you can do
to keep on breathing
to keep on thinking
for your self
never mind having the energy or time
to rise up

failing

Marcus fails every day
hauling his agitated body into work
strung out on the coke and alcohol he had the night before
unable to do his job properly
because the pressure of that job
has made him a drunk and a cokehead

Judith fails every day
because she doesn't take over the 150 calls a day they require
continually getting hauled into HR to get warned about it
but they never replace her
they never send her a final letter of written warning
because they know pushing her to deal with more complex
tasks
rather than employing more controllers to do it on twice as
much
will mean the next one will fail too

Adrian fails
because he constantly gets caught looking out of the window
daydreaming about the mountains he wants to climb
the ones that make the eagle caged in his heart want to break
free from
free from this monotony
become a part of something else something more
than the spreadsheets and reports he gets paid to churn out
which nobody ever looks at

Scott failed
because he got regimented by his time in the Army
and when pushed into filling the recruitment manager roll
couldn't see past the rules the ticks and crosses the visas and
the passports
reducing our courier fleet to men and woman who had to be
legal

rather than the ones before who used to roar wild around the
streets of London
like a bunch of Red Indians out on the plains hunting buffalo
accepting each job like it were a scalp

Supervisor Glyn failed
when the amount of blood and life he'd eaten up
took its toll on his soul
his stroke turning him into a dripping mess
that now sits on a bench of an Aylesbury care home
having his dribbling mouth wiped for him
by the same kind of workers he used to delight in making feel
as small as the thumb of a cockroach

we all fail
they have put failing into us like a second heart
with their overstretched demands and lack of support
it is ours to eat regurgitate eat again then shit out

only after you have flushed all of what they give you
away
what you have left over
that is you
the glory of our failed lives

but if nothing is left of them
after you have flushed it all away

if you can remain happy
and she still loves you

if you can work out a way
to do it without them

then you have achieved something

where the blood and the bone can be seen

it's not the stamina that these men show
coming in every day for years
only to be nipped at and pulled at
like bait in a shark pool
that I can't fathom

it's not the anxiety that these men have learnt to live with
seeing their colleagues marched into HR
for no apparent reason other than to 'keep them on their toes'
whether or not
it will be them next
that I can't fathom

it's not the cheek-turning swallowing of rage
that these men seem to have mastered
putting up with the constant onslaught
of being made to feel worthless
by supervisors who act like dogs
who need to piss on a man every half-hour
just to remind him that this is their territory
that I can't fathom

it's not even the camaraderie they show
breaking the ice after a colleague
on the back of a particularly nasty bollocking
can't do anything
but sit there
stunned
trying to digest the insults and threats
somebody finally squeezing him on the shoulder
telling him

don't you mind that prick mate
he's only taking it out on you
because his missus keeps asking him if it's in or not
whenever he lays on top of her

causing the whole control room
to crack up in forced laughter
mending that wound stitching back up
the openness where the blood and the bone can be seen
so that they can all carry on working
carry on breathing
for a little while longer together

no
that's not what I can't fathom

what it is
is why none of these men
have never thrown down their headsets
got up from their chairs
and stormed down to the workshop
to pick up a steel wrench
only to come back
and smash it over that supervisor's head
again and again and again
until there is no life left in him
either

that's
what I can't fathom

Hal was right

the IT guys rock
with their £4 coffees and green drinks
littered around their desks
pulling us in to ask us what we think an algorithm is
trying to plumb our minds
see if they can uncover the missing link
that will finally make their new automated allocating system
work
Marcus telling them that it's the fear of death
like what Hal did to that human left on that spaceship
them tapping away at iMacs we only got to purr over
strolling around the Apple store half-drunk on a Saturday
morning
running our hands over them
like we used to run our hands over a woman

the IT guys rock
they are building a new Empire
full of pings and code
they have holographic images of the future
swirling around inside their heads
where everything is connected
by binary code and no people
but that doesn't matter to them
only the vision does

the IT guys rock
they stroke Yorkshire Terriers sat in their laps
to satisfy their emotions
they eat raw fish
like you and me eat pies
they are awkward around people
because their ultimate aim
is to do away with people
they get paid so much

that time means nothing to them
everything is a hobby or a project
all of the blood and anxiety we have
they are trying to rid us of it
they want to make the world a better place
more profitable
less messy

and they say that this is the future
that nothing can stop it
that our jobs will be lost to this
like the metal ticket-machine of a bus conductor
the way she turned its handle
and you'd hear all of those gears and cogs turning around inside
there
before she used those metal teeth to tare that ticket off and hand
it you
was lost to the Oyster card

the IT guys rock
and Hal was right
nothing is more important now
than a number
fed into a machine

the sun bears witness

when our weeks are done
we go back to our flats with two bottles of wine and four beers
in a bag
we come in dirty with work with minds that are still away at
work
with hands ready to pull open those beers and pour them
down our eager throats
wanting to sit beside our windows and watch the sun go down
the same sun
we stuck our chests out at on the walk home
drinking up its warmth letting the last sunbeams of it hit us hit
our hands
that are all tapped out
hit our backs
that are old and crooked from all of the years spent sitting in
the same position
bent over desks tapping away at buttons
sending instructions down to couriers to drive at over 90-
miles-an-hour along a motorway
so that they can deliver a piece of material into the hands of a
CEO's wife
just so she can lunch with her girlfriends without feeling ugly
that same sun that causes the construction worker to sweat
as he feeds his family lifting bricks up and down a ladder all
day
helping to build another block of luxury flats on the site of
another reclaimed youth centre
another shut down library another repossessed playground
that same sun
that the homeless man bakes under that the alcoholic can't
face
that the woman with mental health issues stands at the bus
stop under
putting her hand out to stop every bus that comes along
but never getting on any one of them

the warmth of that sun
that we feel on our faces when we burst out of that door at the
end of another week
that sun
now almost gone from the sky
as we drink wine and beers watching it set
which spends all day bearing witness
to what all of the men and all of the women
have to live under

Underneath

God will not save us we are from Underneath
His hands have been turned to shape a different valley
silicon greenbacks and the wise selling us short before
dumping us
Underneath it has always been the same
always only one last chance
always only the love or the drugs
the music or the poems
Instagram or Netflix
uppers or downers
glory or depression
all somehow enough to get us through
stop us from rising
keep us tied to this council flat stump

intricate plans of escape get formed but their fruition evades
us
we are from Underneath
we have clods for brains
we knock them about in silly postcode wars
toughing it out for our skin-colour
our infiltrated memories and weekend allegiances
our avatars reflected back into the world
more important than the hands we used to hold they say
all of it foam atop of the sea
Underneath our broken bones and torn-out tongues thread
the cement of their structures to keep them sturdy
nothing changes Underneath
only sometimes the flags move about in the air a bit fiercer
and the songs get sung from a different mouth
than the one we all used to share

before we break bread
let me tell you what's said
about those from Underneath
they are bereft of intellect
blind to the craft
they don't know a consonant from a vowel
every scattering of letters ends up in the word CUNT
I'll leave it up to you to decide
what the fuck they mean by that!

they move Underneath they do
so the Media say
like witches gathered around a cauldron
always got a scam going on always an angle
but it's never as clean and simple as it seems
Underneath
single mothers have to be like Hyenas
with their teeth bared
ready to snap and pull at any meat they can

we weren't imprisoned
no one was trying to put a noose around our necks
we didn't have to be in doors by 9 o'clock
football had been taken away from us on the terraces
but we could still sit in any seat on the bus
and we were right royally compensated
with free music and cheap films pumped into our rooms 24/7
it was easy living
sometimes we couldn't even work out if we lived Underneath
or not
and that's when we started to lose our voice

sometimes
you couldn't even put two bits of bread together
to make them a sandwich
sometimes you couldn't put a chicken wing on the table
but you told them
as though it was something to be proud of
that they were from Underneath
through wine-glistening eyes

it was getting closer to Christmas
I needed the money
so I got me mum to set up a meeting with the Provi man
so that I could lend a bag of sand
we sat on the stairs of her flat
he got me to sign his tablet
then handed me over the cash
Christmas is easy Underneath
it's the rest of the year that's hard

they keep offering it you
email after email text after text
you know it's wrong to respond
the lovely lady would be enraged
but there's this lust in you that wants it
needs that hit of what it's like to feel free again
so you do it
have a great couple of weeks buying Comte and avocados
getting her hair cut and drinking better wine
Underneath debt is worse than infidelity
you can run away from one but the other one
it will follow you around forever

it's not to be made light of
it can destroy some families
constantly Underneath it can
it starts with an individual first
they go rotten and once that rot sets in
everything else starts to fall apart
crumbles disintegrates
bruises start to appear first
then a tooth or two goes missing
but there are always those who are constantly crackerjacking
always trying to carve a laugh out of thin air
their constant smiles and cynical look-what-they've-fucking-
done-to-us-now humour
soothes the helpless pain
brings sunshine when there's only rain
and their indomitable spirits
can sometimes make you feel
that you're never gonna have to give up again

if you didn't know it already
you learn that you are from Underneath
when you go for that promotion
when you are told by the Directors
that though your 30 years of experience is important
they have decided to give it to somebody else
a clone who hasn't spent one minute inside a control room
but who's wardrobe and performance
was better than mine

you can tell us what you want
we know what we know
you can shout at us and scream at us
we'll have trouble hearing you up there .
you can spit on us and piss on us
we have resolved to carry on
you can even shit on us
we'll sweep such mess away

you can tell us what you want
we know what we know

Underneath it has always been the same

the first casualty of lockdown

April 2020

Janey calls me up on Teams
she's in a state
she received an email in from HR last night
telling her that she's gonna be laid off
because the company needs to keep an eye on the wage bill
to ensure it remains a going concern
once lockdown passes
they might be able to reemploy her in the future
but need to see how things develop
or don't develop

I tell her I didn't know about it
but thought that something like this was coming
not just for her
but for the many

Janey starts pouring out words that feel like questions
how she's worried about what she'll do
for the food money the rent
how her little two will cope
she's already started feeling the urge to self-harm again
and when the job money goes
she doesn't know if she'll be able
to navigate around all of those forms
waiting in DWP limbo
waiting at the food bank
while the fridge remains empty
and she descends back into that fog

I don't know what to say to her

though the Thames has welcomed back its first dolphins
and the smog has lifted from over San Francisco Bay
and though the flora and fauna seem to be erupting again
the sky is dark
and from over the horizon
there is coming soon the biggest storm
we have ever seen
one no correctly filled out form
will be able to contain

I decide at this stage that it's probably best
to sympathise instead
because those wolves at the DWP
are gonna eat this one up as a snack

a job that makes you cry

May 2020

Demi calls me up on Teams
she is in tears
she needs to log off she says
it is 7.30 in the morning on our 54th day of working from
home trying to pull together all of the test kit collections from
care homes and people having to self-isolate at home
and I'm not wearing any clothes
but I have the wherewithal about me to untick the video link
on Teams
before I sit down in front of the screen to ask her why
she doesn't want to explain
I tell her it's okay to go that I'll let everyone know
she feels guilty then wants to explain
it was this man from a care home she says
I answered the phone and he just started screaming at me
telling me he's been waiting for his collection of tests for two
days
that three people died last night and that I had a lot to answer
for
I asked him for the postcode of his care home so I could check
but when I put it in the system there wasn't even a booking in
there for it
and then he just kept on screaming and shouting about dead
people over and over at me

I tell her not to worry
that I'm getting these types of calls in all the time
that the people organising all of this
give our number out
so that we have to pick up all of the pieces and they don't get
smeared in shit
it's not his fault I tell her
they have no one else to blame
for the abandonment they feel
and the people they care for
dying all around them

it's not fair she says

I know I say back

I haven't the heart to tell her that she is lucky
not to have been furloughed
because when all this is over
those ones won't even have a job left
that makes them cry

working from home

June 2020

Marcus has been working for the last 9 weeks from out of his flat
helping to keep together the collections of covid test kits and
distribution of PPE equipment
from all of the care homes and to all of the hospitals and drive
through test centres
across the country

the tools he's been given
to make this happen
are a rented Compaq laptop
a 5-year-old Dell 13-inch monitor
a headset with a microphone attached to it
that he's had to tape to keep in place
and an operating system that keeps dropping off his internet
connection

from 7am to 11pm every day
for 62 days solid now
he's logged on
using this equipment
to keep up with the onslaught of emails coming in from the
Administrators who have been employed ████████████ to
coordinate the nationwide fight
to contain this virus

Administrators who request collections of administered test kits
from care homes
that Marcus knows
haven't even received
their outbound yet
to the onslaught
of emails wanting him to organise 34 long-wheel-base vans
to collect pallets of PPE from a warehouse in Oxfordshire

to go to hospitals and drive through test centres
that he knows will not be ready when they get there
or leave light
when they finally are

to the onslaught
of calls coming in from care home staff
wanting to know why their test kits haven't been collected yet
that it's been a week now
since they had their last courier
which after he's checked
can see on the system
that there's not even been a request from the Administrators
emailed in for them yet
them finally giving up
telling him not to bother
because another one of them died overnight
so the whole home must be riddled with it
and to experience
once again
his 5-year-old boy
pulling at his t-shirt for attention
turning to his mother
sitting on the couch
blankly staring off through the depression
that's anchored itself around her head
like an irremovable fog
asking her why daddy
loves his phone more than him
now

damaged goods

June 2020

Leamington pulls me aside
says he needs to talk to me
we go into the interview room off the control room
it is quite in there and there is cool air that our unmasked
faces suck in
it feels like I'm in a spa!

we sit on a chair each
two meters apart
I look at him
wait for him to start what it is he's pulled me aside for

he sits forward on his chair elbows on his knees
his head in his hands
staring at the floor
saying nothing

the stillness of it all is off-putting

he rubs his right hand all over his head and then his face then
leans back and looks at me

what's wrong, I say

I don't know
things have changed
I've got this anger inside me that never existed before

before what, I say

before lockdown, he says
oh, lockdown, I say

yeah I'm not the same anymore
I get angry real quick and I'm worried it's coming out when
I'm doing my job
talking to the couriers and customers
I can't deal with their *little issues*
they can't find this address can't find that address
where's my courier why's it so late
I just want to tell them all to fuck off
and leave me alone

I tell him about how my lady attacked me in fourth week of
lockdown
went for me with a wooden spoon and a colander because the
phone wouldn't stop ringing
and there was always something to attend to
other than her
from 7am to midnight
care home this PPE that
no time for her
when before
the job was all done away from home
there was a certain distance
that kept everything remote
and the money coming in felt clean
it became a bit like having to wring a chicken's neck
before you got to eat it
rather than buying it in a supermarket
already wrapped up in plastic
bringing all of that killing into the home
she couldn't take the intensity of it
the act of the production of money
dirtied and confused everything
and then when she snapped
she came at me with that colander and spoon
started banging them both on my head

he laughs
says he knows what I mean
how did you deal with it, he asks

I just put it down to lockdown
started wearing that colander on my head
and tucking that wooden spoon out the back of my pants
so she could see
that I was ready for her

he laughs again

I just wanted you to know
that if I seem different then it's not me but all that I've gone
through

even though I knew that the two were the same thing
I told him that it's okay
to come find me
if ever he feels like murdering something again

he says thanks before we put our masks back up
and enter back out into the noise heat and stale air of the
control room

when the supervisors finally decide
that it's safe for them to come back in
safe again for them to sit on the tube
along with the rest of us
and begin once again
prowling around the control room
looking for meat to eat
he won't last five-minutes
before being signed off
as damaged goods

lockdown abuse

April to July 2020

At 10.30 every morning there is a Teams call. Everyone invited must join. It doesn't matter what you are doing. You could be routing 6000 care homes, have a matron on the phone wanting to know where her test kits are, a front of house from a private hospital trying to book a major hemorrhage courier to bring blood from the lab as quickly as possible, or the kid could be screaming and going mental in the background because its iPad won't stream YouTube quickly enough.

Whatever it was, you had to drop it and be on that call at 10:30 sharp. If not then the Generals would get the hump, they'd see it as a sign of disrespect. They wouldn't say so on the call, but you could tell, the way they'd drop the usual 'hello' and just say your name all surprised like when you finally joined. Then later, when you were back on the laptop helping to try and keep it all together, one of the Lesser Generals would call you up and tell you that the Greater Generals noted that you were 12-minutes late to join the call. You explain to the Lesser General that you were in the middle of speaking to someone from the Administrators about a potentially missing pallet of PPE needed at the Edinburgh Infirmary. Nevertheless, the Lesser General will say, it's been noted, you were late on the call and they're not happy about it.

When you put the phone down on the Lesser General you go into your kid's bedroom grab the iPad and smash it against the wall. Instantly the noise stops. For 5 or 10 seconds you let the silence ease its jet of warm water all over your mind. Then soon after that the guilt starts...

slowly breaking apart

July 2020

Chloe has spent the last 14-weeks in her bedsit above the Spar
on Kilburn High Road answering phones that constantly ring
in on the laptop the company gave her when lockdown was
announced – her 6-year-old son is with her – the school is
shut and she has no family to take him off her hands – he
watches her mother work taking calls in from care home staff
and isolated workers stuck in homes 14 times bigger than
Chloe's all demanding to know why their test kits haven't been
collected yet – and I can see Chloe calling me up on Teams as
I am on another call talking to the Matron of a care home in
Sunderland – after I have dealt with the Sunderland issue I call
Chloe back – she tells me she had a woman on the phone from
a care home in Plymouth spitting at her wanting to know
when her test kits were going to be collected – I don't ask
Chloe for the post code so that I can check when they will be
collected – or even if the Administrators have emailed an
order in for them yet – I ask her how she is instead – she says
that she is doing shit – that her son has started screaming a lot
for no apparent reason – that she feels lost and isolated – not
isolated in the covid sense – just fucking isolated – like she is
in a prison and someone has thrown away the key – and as we
talk on Teams together we can both see the calls coming in –
there are only 16 of us dealing with all of this – the others
having been furloughed or assigned to other tasks – we wish
each other good luck before departing and getting back down
to answering the phones trying to help keep it all together as
the 6-year-old's scream and the Chloe's above the Spar's in
Kilburn and everywhere else
slowly break apart...

the doors have been opened for Leamington

July 2020

Leamington is not the same since he returned from lockdown
that wide smile full of teeth and cheeky mischievous eyes
they're gone
replaced by a tightly screwed up pair of lips
below sleepy dull eyes

everything about Leamington before was turned out
out towards the world
which he greeted with joy and enthusiasm
but now
it has all been turned around
and faces in
the heat of those smiles and eyes burning him up inside

lockdown was not kind to him
lost two relations
and furloughed spent 3 months looking within
or at the walls
churning over the losses in his head
the on-top-of-each-other-all-the-fucking-time sniping and
nipping with his lady
the rows and hurtful sentences
that came out of her mouth

not even needed by work
you fucking waste of space
sleep till 10, fuck me, I wish I had nothing to do with my life
that I could sleep till 10

the snap came suddenly and from out of nowhere
smashing up their flat and putting all the windows in
a sudden purge 9 weeks in
to scour out all of the bitterness awakened in him
thought that'd be it then
outted
but once the big doors have been opened
they always remain ajar
and nothing is ever the same again

at lunch he doesn't socially distance with anyone in the
lunchroom
for small talk and jokes anymore
attends therapy sessions on Zoom instead
to discuss the lockdown
the effects it's had on him
why he now feels so angry all the time
and enjoys
absolutely nothing about himself

5 litres of Adblue

August 2020

nothing was going through his mind
sat inside that 'much-needed' van of his
outside that warehouse that had become his second home
over the last four months
waiting for them to pick & pack then roll out
his 'much-needed' load of PPE

the deep amber lights illuminating the forecourt
had become his new night-light
so he tried to get some sleep
but too tired it wouldn't come

booked for ten it was
but now
one in the morning
he started getting fidgety
thinking of the miles he'd have to drive –
when they eventually rolled out his 'much-needed' loads of PPE –
to the hospitals in Glasgow Edinburgh Perth
and Inverness

the loading bay was empty
not a warehouseman in sight
three hours now it'd been
waiting there
when he thought he'd help himself
to a top-up of Adblue from the driver's pump

so he got his jerrycan and helped himself
to what his 'much-needed' van needed to get through those miles
his was a wrap of speed but unfortunately
his 'much-needed' van wouldn't run on such chemicals alone

bent over there pumping it in
they suddenly appeared
two warehouseman and the foreman

what are you doing the foreman said

Adblue he said the van needs it

you can't be stealing our Adblue

stealing? he said

yes the Adblue is for ▮▮▮ drivers and ▮▮▮ vans only

come on he said I've been picking up PPE from here for four
months now
give me a break

the foreman made him pour it back in the tank

words were exchanged

it was midday when the email came in from the
Administrators
one of our drivers had been caught stealing Adblue from the
Banbury warehouse
and when challenged had become aggressive
sworn at the staff there
there was no way they could accept such behaviour
so they didn't want him on site
or collecting from there anymore
when he called in empty from Inverness
he was told that he'd lost his job

four months driving up and down the country
delivering 'much-needed' PPE to all the hospitals
and drive through test centres
in his 'much-needed' van
being there back in April when it was all full-on
when no one had a mask or a pair of gloves
taking on more and more of whatever it was that was needed
driving through hours and nights that turned into early
mornings
all
forgotten
for £5.50's worth of Adblue

must've been the longest drive back he'd ever taken on

153 days in

August 2020

I'm tired of being tough
I'm tired of taking it all on
I'm tired of rolling up my sleeves
and charging against all of their walls
I'm tired of clearing up
the lost PPE the misplaced test kits
the invisible aprons and masks
I'm tired of having to make up excuses to hospital staff
why the vans have delivered light
I'm tired of the days the nights
sifting through all of their emails
as they sit in their underfloor-heated palaces
pinging them off
it is like ordering sushi on Deliveroo for them
I'm tired of trying to piece together what they want
how it can be done
I'm tired of putting what has fallen apart
back together again
I'm tired of answering the phone
to care home staff
telling me not to bother delivering all 50 test kits now
that 45 will do
because 5 of them died overnight
I'm tired of that
I'm tired of having to send that through my head night after
night
I'm tired of juggling speaking feeling witnessing
the mess
I'm tired of the mess
every day I get up
and have to try and clean up their mess
that is what I am tired of
their mess

it is too big to clean up now

how it is for them

September 2020

Sophie is all in a sweat
she works for the Administrators and gets paid a percent
of the overall budget
if everything goes smoothly
she is in a sweat because she has a VIP who needs a test done
quick
I tell her that the VIP's in trouble then because from what I've
heard
the Government website keeps coming up with NO
AVAILABILITY when trying to book a test
she says not to worry about that
that she's got two tests boxed-up and ready to collect
from the reception of the Department of Health building in
Victoria Street
that what she needs is a courier
to pick them up and drive them straight down to Somerset
where he'll have to wait outside the family home while the
tests are done
then whizz them back up to the ███████████ in ███████
███████
I tell her
I don't think that's the best use of our resources at the moment
but Sophie insists
she knows what'll get her percent paid into her bank account
so I pull a courier off his care home run and tell him to get to
Victoria Street quick

230 miles later he pulls up outside the VIP's house
it is a lonely house fully detached
there is a plumb tree on the lawn
a field pours out towards the Atlantic to its right
he hands over the kits to the lady at the door
then waits

after 45-minutes a different lady appears at the door
Portuguese beckons him over to take from her the
administered kits

274 miles later he pulls into the delivery yard of the BioCentre
Lab in Milton Keynes where the kits are taken from him and
rushed in to be tested

this Test & Trace system might not be working for you
but for ███████████ VIPs
it's working like a dream

how it is for Stella

September 2020

Stella is in a sweat
she works for a courier company as a telephonist
the last 3 months she's been locked down in her flat
sat at a table in her kitchen answering phones via the laptop
her 8-year-old and 4-year-old's school has been shut
so they've been crawling and marauding around all over the
place
making noise jumping up and down fighting and screaming

Stella gets an email in every night from her supervisor
a report letting her know how many calls she's taken
how far she is off her targets
why is she 20 calls down on her target?
does she need to be furloughed?

Stella doesn't want to be furloughed
because when the cull starts
she knows that the furloughed will be the first ones to be laid off

Stella's heart leaped
when the schools announced that they'd be opening up again
next week
both of them could start back just disappear like they used too
it doesn't matter for some working mothers what they learn
it only matters that they get the space so that they can go out and
earn
and she's smashing it now
35 calls above her target each day
the supervisor is obviously happy
because she doesn't even bother sending her emails anymore

then last Friday the school called
the 8-year-old has been coughing and sneezing in class
she needs to come and collect her
get her a test before she's allowed to attend again
and because the 4-year-old lives in the same flat
she needs to go too

the Government website keeps on saying NO AVAILABILITY
NO AVAILABILITY
unless she's willing to drive to Swindon or Dundee

the crawling and marauding around all over the flat
the noise the fighting and the screaming
start up again

and then her calls drop

and then the emails start coming in

now furloughing is not an option
she is an inch away from getting laid off
unless she can get a test and clear her kids to go back to school
so that she can concentrate on the calls again

this Test & Trace system might be working for them
but for a telephonist locked down in a flat with two kids
causing mayhem
trying to hit targets so that she can keep hold of her job
it's not working for her

another day on the care home shift

September 2020

Sabrina gets the call – it is Mrs Frostrop
Head of Operations for the Berkeley Care Home Syndicate
they manage 134 care homes around the country
80% of their staff are subbed out
called in when needed
4-hours here 4-hours there
they move between care homes like a virus
squeezing full Tennas and colostomy pouches out like they
were old tea bags
filling in the gaps left behind by the outsourcing explosion
everyone is Agency now – even music and poetry

we've got to know her well over the last 16 weeks since
lockdown
having to work this operation from out of our front rooms
Mrs Frostrop
she is the shrapnel of the system
she is Adolph Hitler's daughter
you can smell her swastikas down the phone when she's onto
you
wanting to know where her Randox kits are for The Blue Blush
Care Home in Hastings
where her Kingfisher kits are for the Pine Ridge Retirement
Centre in Whitley Bay

Sabrina working from home sat in her bedsit above the
CostCutter on Harrow Rd with her 5-year-old tugging at her t-
shirt for attention
she is unsure what to say to her
she calls me up on Teams says Mart I've got Frosty Drop on
the phone again wanting to know where kits are
I tell her to put her through to me
she asks how do I do that

I start to explain and halfway through Sabrina tells me not to
worry
she's hung up
she will come back within 30 seconds though I know that
that is how she is made like a dog who won't give up even when
it knows it can't win

I watch the call board on my laptop from my flat
I haven't got a 5-year-old anymore – I've only got a wife I've
ignored for 100 days
she was okay with it all for the first few weeks but then gradually
she gathered up the listening of me going on and on on the
phone from 6am to midnight into a weather pattern that then
turned into a storm which then turned into a gale which then
turned into a hurricane which now has anchored itself over her
head and pushes her along with it into deep low bouts of
aggressive depression

I have to watch my back when I occasionally leave my chair
to go to the toilet or get a drink
she has come at me recently with various household implements
a wooden spoon a colander an iron and a butter knife just in the
last week
we haven't kissed or held hands for a month

then I see Frostrop's number pop up on the display
no one answers it – they all have it written down on the pad of
their minds
there's an X by it
don't answer that one the X says
so I get it

Zeig Heil Zeig Heil she says
I ask her for the postcodes of the care homes she is enquiring
about
after a few more Zeig Heils she gives me them
I enter them into our operating system
but they aren't there I can't find them

which means that we haven't received a booking to collect from them from the Administrators hired by ███████ ██████████ ██████ who run this operation – they are accountants – lives lost don't mean anything to them as long as they can audit the loss properly

a little butterfly rises up inside my lungs and before it can come out of my mouth it is an eagle

I tell her sorry Mrs Fistdrop but we don't have an order for Blue Blush or Pine Ridge in our system
Zeig Heil Zeig Heil
you need to call this number who are the Administrators of it all
Zeig Heil Zeig Heil
it is ███
Zeig Heil Zeig Heil
we only deal with orders that we have received and cannot do anything about orders to collect or deliver test kits that we haven't received yet through the proper channels
Zeig Heil Zeig Heil
then she puts the phone down on me

40-minutes later we get an email in from the Administrators ordering two urgent vans to collect 50 test kits each from the ██████ warehouse in ██████████ where all of it is stored
and get them to The Blue Blush Care Home in Hastings and Pine Ridge Retirement Centre in Whitley Bay
as quickly as possible

this is how it works
everything is reactionary
whoever makes the most noise gets listened to first
no one knows what is going on

tomorrow will be the same

and then the next day
more infected
more dead

on the menu today

October 2020

7352 care home collections between 4 and 9pm

174 GP and dentist collections between 9 and 1pm

146 prison collections between 6 and 9pm

245 Mobile Test Units
to be collected within a one-hour window between 12 and
1pm

174 pallets of PPE
to collect from a ▓▓▓▓ warehouse in ▓▓▓▓▓▓▓▓▓ in 30-
minute slots
before having to be delivered to all of the MTUs and hospitals
around the country

286 pre-booked RTS collections
all to be collected within a 30-minute window
having to deliver them then
directly into one of the five privately owned labs

356 Elective Surgery collections
straight from patient's homes into the labs
so that they can be tested to see if they are clear
for emergency operations they've waited months for

a network of 18-ton trucks collecting in the early hours of
each morning from all of the delivery depots ferrying in all of
the test kits collected the previous day to one of the five
privately owned labs

the constant debilitating drain of dealing with incoming calls
from any interested party of any of the above demanding to
know the status of their deliveries or collections
people from the Administrators working their 3-weeks 'on the
programme' wanting to divert vans 5-minutes from the ███████
███████ lab to the ███████ lab because ███████████████ is
maxed out with tests and won't catch up for 36-hours

and just 16 of us with compulsory invites to sit at the table
some for 15-hours a day
all others having been denied access to eat through the
furloughing scheme

for months we've been fed this

with no indigestion tablets supplied

with no adequate napkins to wipe up the mess

with the same menu and same seating plan set for tomorrow

a feast that never seems to end

the menu that never seems to change

the bill to be picked up by not only our daughters and sons
but theirs also

sending him down to Crabble Hill

December 2020

full of life and enthusiasm as usual
he called me up to log on for work
how's it looking today boss he said
busy I said
that's good he said I'm ready for whatever it is you've got for me
you've got 4 emergency collections around Gillingham then a
care home route down around Dover later on this evening I said
perfect he said I'm ready to leave now
so I used my fingertips to press the buttons that sent the work
down to him

his schedule for the day was now locked

a couple of hours later I checked his progress on the GPS
he was on schedule
he was always on schedule
he was someone I could always rely on
could always count on to care enough to make it happen

on the 18th care home collection of his 25-address route
he tried to pull into the Crabble Hill care home on the A256
Dover Road
but the gate was shut
and the buzzer seemed to not be working
so he backed out and reversed into the lay-by on the other side of
the road

getting out he crossed the road only to find a lady from the care
home waiting at the gate ready to hand him over the test kits
sorry about the gate she said it's been playing up all week
that's okay he said no trouble
I saw you from the reception so I thought I'd bring them out to
you she said

that's a big box he said
yes she said we tested all 87 of them this morning
great
better get them off to the lab for you as quickly as possible then
he said
ahh you're an angel she said before handing them over to him

30-seconds later
a grey Ford Focus sped around the corner
mounted the pavement
and ran him down

the Ford Focus drove off
leaving him to die at the scene
turned straight into an angel like the lady from the care home
said
and disappeared into the sky

in times of tragedy
you trace the lines of responsibility back
back to where it all started
when it all started
trying to work out the how's and the why's
but the timelines become blurry
the further you go back
leaving you feeling responsible
for it happening on your watch
because your fingertips were undeniably
the ones that sent him down to Crabble Hill

Christmas Day is a lie

December 2020

Working on Christmas Day, we got a call in from the head-honcho at the ▆▆ who is responsible for the coordination and all the logistics of the fight to contain this thing. He is a ▆▆ employee really, just been implanted into the ▆▆ and given a ▆▆ email address so that it all looks smoother and less outsourced. I've spoken to him before – a complete shit-shifter who doesn't know his Edinburgh's from his St Albans. He was in a state – needed our help to clear all the test-kits taken by the roadside from all of the truck drivers stuck at Dover trying to get back over to the continent. They'd managed to get them all together in a hangar at Manston Airport in Ramsgate but had forgotten to arrange transport for them to get to the actual lab so that they could be tested. A potential front-pager he must've thought, better put my glass of champagne down and get involved. So he got on the phone and told me that we needed to supply three 7.5-ton trucks to collect the used and unused test kits from Manston Airport and take them out to ▆▆ ▆▆ at Heathrow where a flight had been specially laid on to fly them over to ▆▆ where the ▆▆ lab, which was going to test them, is. Obviously finding three 7.5-ton trucks in the Ramsgate area on Christmas Day is not an easy task. I don't think he would've appreciated me telling him to use a few of the thousands of lorries parked up empty on the motorway trying to get on a ferry out of Dover – though the thought did cross my mind. After lots of calls we managed to drag three drivers with 7.5-trucks away from their Christmas lunches and head down to Ramsgate. Upon arrival and much security checking of id's and such, each one was given a 60-mile-an-hour siren-blaring police escort across the tarmac to the hangar that contained the kits. There was no one else around within a 5 mile radius. What a palaver. And all because the Administrators our ▆▆ have paid hundreds of millions of pounds to to fight and help contain this thing had forgotten to previously arrange the transport. It's a bit like going on holiday and forgetting to book the cab to take you to the airport. Later we were told that the day after the same guy – the head-honcho – was on Twitter tweeting about how what a marvelous coordinated and organized operation with the ███ it was getting all of those thousands of lorry drivers tested and their tests to the labs so that they could get back to their families and enjoy the rest of their Christmases. Was it hell! The Army, as good a job as they have done throughout this crisis, in this instance they only got the kits from the roadside to the airport hangar – getting the kits the final mile into the airport so that they could be flown over to the ███ lab in ███ was carried out by three men who I had to convince to drag themselves away from their Christmas dinners – mouths still chewing stuffing, a box of mince pies under their arms for the trip – and to get in their vans and drive down to Marsten Airport as quickly as they can.

How about that for a Christmas lie!

Mohammed wants the Army back

January 2021

Mohammed, call sign Charlie134, arrives at the Warrington Mobile Test Unit on time. He has been sent to pick up the administered kits so that he can take them to the ███████████ lab in ████████████ for testing. The Serco guy at the gate asks him for his ID. Mohammed shows him his ID. The Serco guy asks him what the registration number of his vehicle is. Why, Mohammed asks. It's our security question, the Serco guy says, it's a bit like your favourite word question on your Amazon account but this is designed to see if you know what the vehicle is that you're driving. Mohammed tells him it, says DOH! The Serco guy looks at him strangely then lets him in and tells him to go over to the big gazebo over on the left. Mohammed tells him that he knows. He's been collecting from this MTU since it opened when the Army used to run it before the ███████████ farmed it out to Serco.

Mohammed drives over to the big gazebo. A Serco guy suddenly appears from out of nowhere and stands in front of Mohammed's van with his arm held out palm up shouting STOP! Mohammed stops. The Serco guy comes over to Mohammed's driver's window and asks what he's here for. Mohammed tells him that he's here to collect the test kits to take to the lab. The Serco guy hollers out to another Serco guy that there's a van here to collect the kits for the lab. The other Serco guy comes over and says what kits? Mohammed explains – all the tests you've taken today? from all the people? I'm here to pick them up and take them to the lab so that they can be tested. It's what this whole thing is for. The two Serco guys look at each other confused. Do you know where they are one of them asks the other. Nope – but they must be around here somewhere. Then they both disappear behind the big gazebo to look for them.

Thirty minutes later one of the Serco guys reappears and says to Mohammed that they may have a problem. What's that then asks Mohammed. We think we may have given the test kits for the lab to the van that came earlier to pick up all of the refuse. Oh, Mohammed says. The Serco guy disappears again.

Mohammed calls me up on the phone and tells me that they've given the test kits to the rubbish men. I tell him to get one of their names so that we can forward it on to the Administrators to let them know what has happened.

It wasn't like this Mohammed says to me when the Army were running this MTU. I've basically just spent 30-minutes waiting for these guys to tell me that they've given the test kits to the dustmen. Why are these guys even given this responsibility man. Now I am behind on all of my collections and will have the back end of my schedule taken away from me. It's gonna lose me at least 70 or 80 quid. I want the Army back.

Mohammed puts the phone down and it takes a few seconds
before what Mohammed has said to me to register
I smile to myself
as the cash tills ring
and test kits end up in landfill
instead of labs

Serco

perfidious lobbyist, scythe wielder
lopping heads off of jobs while they are still flowers
producing scent, with firm stems
and so much life still left in them
sending them back to the concrete composite heaps of the
discarded
to queue for food
and worry about the rent

corrupted bully, tentacled beast
you have one in every Commons negotiating room
we are cheaper, cheaper we are
you bang all of your hundred fists on the tables at once
the cheapest always wins in these backhanded transactions
where ink is the blood of forgotten citizenship

and then you make it work
cutting quality, services
jobs paying peas, creating margin out of pips
margin that will grow you a billion more fruit trees
all bearing more of the rotten fruit of your rotten schemes

Mohammed Zahida and Mushtaq too

January 2021

the amount of hours these men and women spend sat in their
vans
driving across the country collecting test kits from care homes
it is like they are machines
who never tire
who never give in
running through the tasks we send them
without any moans or gripes
without breaking down or developing faults
their stamina is not natural
it is forged in some faraway place
where graft under the sun opens up the skin
and shows it's only true colour
which is sweat

these men and women
who when walking around our cobbled streets
the ones they share with you and me
are looked down upon by some
sponger dirtbag terrorist scum
but who now
along with others of their kin
are keeping open the arteries of this reclaimed country
allowing its blood still to flow
even though the rest of it
seems to be bent down on its knees

the Partner in the ice cream van

January 2021

the other courier companies we use
to help bring all of this covid work together
we call Partners
they offer their services to us
we couldn't do it without them
the care homes are from Penwith to John O'Groats
the MTUs from Aberdeen to Penzance
it needs a nationwide coordinated response
which we have had to set up privately
because our ▮▮▮▮▮▮▮ couldn't do it

we email them what we can't do
to see if they can do it
they never say no
it's always a yes
they have people in vans
almost everywhere

one day last week
we had a complaint in from the Administrators
wanting to know why an ice-cream van
turned up at the MTU in Perth
wanting to collect the test kits

apparently it drove in to the MTU with ice-cream music blaring
pulling up next to the gazebo
the driver not getting out
but going to the hatch at the back
before leaning out and loudly announcing
that he was there to collect the test kits
after the initial shock and checking of his courier id
the Serco guys handed him through the hatch
two MeDX boxes filled with administered kits

which he stacked on the shelf at the back
beside the raspberry and chocolate sauces
before turning back to the Serco guys and saying

right then lads, anyone fancy a 99
or an oyster with a flake

I don't think their criteria
for taking on couriers
is as stringent as ours

but it couldn't be done without them

the repatriation of the strawberry milkshake powder

February 2021

the courier sent to the Sunny Bay View care home in Whitley
Bay couldn't find anyone in the reception area to help him locate
the box of test kits he'd been sent there to collect

so he had a rummage around
he poked his nose inside the cupboard by the lift
he looked behind the plants next to the fish tank
he peered into the reception room
and when he saw a box there that he thought contained the covid
test kits
that were supposed to have been administered to the residents
the evening before
he loaded it into the back of his van and carried on with the rest
of his collections

it was only upon delivery at the ▮▮▮▮▮▮▮ lab in ▮▮▮▮▮▮▮
when it was discovered that the box the courier had picked up
contained 6 cartons of strawberry milkshake powder
that we were we called

a big furore ensued
the ▮▮▮▮▮▮▮▮▮▮ were notified who in turn notified the
Administrators who in turn got their Director of Operations to
call our Director of Operations demanding to know what had
happened
that we had better get that box of strawberry milkshake powder
picked up from the lab as quickly as possible
and returned to the Sunny Bay View care home in Whitley Bay
before anyone cottons on to what has happened

back in April
it was okay for them to leave thousands of care home
residents dying in their rooms
but now
now that their PR machine is in full swing
fully functioning and designed to head off any potential
embarrassments
mitigating and proportioning blame along the way
the repatriation of that strawberry milkshake powder
was of paramount importance

the forgotten neighbour

the neighbour who lives under me
got in the way when I was carrying the rubbish out on Boxing
Day
he was on the landing
in his Miami-coloured shorts and dirty white vest-top
leaning on his stroller
his electric is off
he wants to know if it is the same in my flat
he wants to know if I've ever killed a man
or a woman
he is in the early stages of dementia
confused as a red setter
the colour of his eyes are just about visible under shallow water
like stones in a river
they are cold and black he is
life in its first death throes

but it's Christmas
so I go in to see why he hasn't any electricity – there is a meter
it is a key affair – I ask him when he last topped up – he
is outside on the landing leaning on his stroller – I open the door
ask him – 'when did you last top up?'
he can't remember – he thinks
the Germans are coming up the stairs
all of the fight in him has been
internalised
lost
lost

I think for a second that right now
I could kill him
I could just bundle him back into his flat
and lay on top of him until he stopped breathing
who would know?
who would care?

but it's Christmas
so I take his key up to Kilburn instead
put a score on it then come back
stick it in the meter and make sure his heat is on
I check his fridge
he has nothing in there but old milk
an open packet of bacon
and the broken half
of an Easter egg

if someone else had caught him on the landing
say in mid-January
skint and desperate
after spending everything they had on Christmas
they could've killed him
put him out of his misery
stolen his half of Easter egg

no one would've known
no one would've cared

the neighbour and the light bulb

the neighbour underneath me is at my door
he wants to know if I have a spare lightbulb
it is 2pm on a Saturday afternoon
and he is dying of dementia

so I give him a lightbulb
I don't ask if it's a screw in one or a twist he needs
it's not like he's actually going to use it
he just takes it from me
and says thank you

as I hand it over to him at the door
he looks at me
turns his head from side to side
like a dog
then he says
did you come round mine at Christmas?

there's still life in there

no, I tell him, I met you on the landing on Boxing Day
your electricity was off

electricity? oh, yes

he doesn't know what the hell I'm on about

where do I go from here, he says

in the lift taking him back down to his floor
I can smell the death he holds my hand with
he calls me Andrew
his fingers are like the penis bones of a primate
hard and wanting to break through the thinnest skin

when I get him in his flat
it is a wasteland
no signs of recent life
no photos
no order
there is a kettle on the mantelpiece
a loo roll on the floor
an open packet of Wotsits on the windowsill
everything is exactly where it was left
when it was last touched
weeks or maybe even months ago

he sits in his chair
I place a glass of water beside him and switch on the tele
Love Island is on

thank you, Andrew, he says

I don't say anything

the whole world is humming outside
and sometimes it is hard to understand why

the neighbour and the flood

there's a knock at the door
before I open it I know it is him
the forgotten neighbour
trying to be unforgotten

I open the door
yes
it's him again

have you got a leak, he says
no, I don't think so, I say

that's funny, he says
because there's water all over my floors

I tell him to stay there
and I jump down the stairs
but his door is shut
so I jump back up them again
and tell him that his front door is shut
he says, what door

I ask him if he has the key
he says, what key

shit, I say, the key to your flat
what flat, he says

the one you live in that my flat is leaking water into?
oh, that flat, he says

he tweezers his fingers into his neck and pulls out of the puffy
water-retented fat of his neck a bit of string that raises a key up
out of his dirty white vest-top

somebody still cares
somebody did that

or maybe he did it in a moment of clarity
knowing that he'd find himself in this position again

I take the key from him
jump down the stairs
put it in and open up the door
expecting water to be everywhere

but there is nothing

I check the kitchen, front room and bathroom

nothing

I go into his bedroom
nothing
no water
but beside his bed
there is a photo of a lady smiling
eating candy floss on a pier
and there are the letters M A V I S
written in black bingo pen above it on the wall

when I go back up I tell him that I've cleaned it all up and that I
will get a plumber in to make sure that it doesn't happen again

he says, thank you Andrew
you're a good boy

the neighbour with Red Indian kids

up above
in number 19
there is a pack of Red Indians
who every night when I go to bed
ride their ponies over the prairies of their wooden floors
hunting buffalo

I imagine them
as I lay there not able to sleep
sitting around the campfire together
painting their faces up in war paint
wearing headdresses with eagle feathers in
swinging tomahawks around in their hands
before getting on their ponies and going out to hunt

it can go on for a long time
their hunt
and as I twist and turn
unable to sleep
I think of Geronimo and Cochise
Standing Bear and Big Elk
how they were once stopped from hunting
and incarcerated
by the White Man

in the morning when I'm off out to work
I press the button for the lift
and sometimes it comes down from above
with their mother in it

she looks at me
says sorry for the noise last night

I tell her not to worry

we go down the rest of the floors in silence

I will fall asleep later on the tube
miss my stop
be late in for work

the alternative is worse

the neighbour from number 11

the lady from number 11 bakes cakes
leaves them by my door
she doesn't knock
she just leaves them there
in a big glass dish
with tinfoil wrapped around them

they aren't big cakes
but little bite-sized ones
with crushed pistachios nested
in a sweet sticky glue
on top

it all started a couple of years back
I was walking up the stairs and she was going into her flat
she's smaller than a mole
comes from Iraq her back
is the shape of a mountain
and bent over there with bags of shopping all around her
I asked her if she was okay

she turned around

her eyes were more alive
than her body suggested

yes, she said, you?

I'm fine, I said

you like cakes? she said
I don't particularly like cakes
preferring savory items instead

yes, I said

wait there, she said

then she went into her flat
and brought out a big glass dish filled with cakes

you have, she said

I went to take one but she said no
you take all
bring back dish when finished

I said no I couldn't possibly
but she insisted

so I walked up the rest of the stairs
with that big glass bowl full of cakes in my hands

that was a couple of years ago

now, often when I return home from work
there's that same glass bowl filled with cakes
outside my door

I return the bowl in the morning
when I go off to work again
don't knock
just leave it there
like she does

whenever our paths do cross
in the courtyard
or by the entrance door to our block
she fixes me with those eyes of hers

you enjoy? she asks

yes, I say, very good

sometimes
you have to force kindness into you
so that it can be returned again and again
like a sweet glue
sticking us all together

the cake neighbour

when I bump into the lady from number 11
in the courtyard
or by the entrance door to our block
she asks me how I am

I tell her that I'm good
I ask her how she is
she just raises her shoulders
and makes a face
she's not sure
and I am a liar

she has this way with her eyes
of letting you know
that what she doesn't know
is most probably not even worth knowing

I wonder if she has found some of the cakes she leaves outside
my door
in the communal bin
I tell myself no
but her eyes tell me differently
she is threaded through everything
from the stars to the moon
then back again

she says that I am a good man
she can tell it by the way I spend time with her
discussing nothing
discussing the hand of hers that she recently bruised
she can see it in the palm of my eyes

the lack of anything
that judges or winces

I tell her that I don't know about that
she says that she does

we communicate with our hands and faces for 15-minutes at a
time

she believes in her heart and Allah
I believe in nothing
but her eyes
are two of the most important things in the world to me
and that can be enough
sometimes

the neighbour from number 15

is a hoarder
she once had a dentist's chair outside her front door
and there's always 4 or 5 boxes of sweet nothing out there
waiting to be brought in

she has a little wood going on
on the landing
there are plants flowering yuccas and cactus that have been so
cared for and correctly watered
that they reach up almost to the ceiling

when I walk down the stairs I need a machete to get out
sometimes I don't want to get out
sometimes I do

her balcony is under mine
the smell of rain-soaked rotting cardboard
wafts up onto my balcony in Summer
sometimes it reminds me of that golden time after a long hot day
in between after the earth has just been pounded by a rainstorm
and before when the heat kicks back in again
but most of the time
it reminds me of markets with sewers and rotting fruit in the air

when I bump into her in the courtyard outside
I don't say to her, 'hey! what the fuck's going on with your
hoarding man
you need to clean your shit up woman'

no, I ask her how she's doing

she tells me that she's not doing so well
that her son is trouble and the council haven't been round to fix
her boiler yet
that the man opposite her keeps knocking on her door asking for
lightbulbs
that she is worried about the new people in number 9
always coming and going at all hours making the noise
and how she suspects someone in the block has a dog in there
because all she can hear late at night is all this running about on
the floors
which you know is against the rules don't you?

I leave her 20-minutes later
in the courtyard
which we all have to walk through
to get away from
or return
to all of our stuff

the neighbour from Vietnam in number 15

has had a stroke
she will never walk again
through the courtyard
dragging her thin blue plastic bags full of fish-heads
unsellable veg
discarded fruit
that she forages from the market
in the 30-minutes after it shuts and before the dustmen move in

never again
will she stop me when I'm tired and trying to get back home
from work
to ask me how I am

never again will we tiptoe around the noise my flat gives her
at unpredictable moments
the way her flat sends up her son's outbursts and screams into
mine

never again will we discuss
why the council has done this to her
removed all of her plants
and ceremonial ceramic waterfalls
which she had cultivated over the years
like a perfect Japanese garden
off the landing
'because they are a fire risk!?
coming on, pfft'

fucking idiots, I agree with her

she is in Charring Cross Hospital now
just off a life-support machine
her brother tells me that she can't use her arms
that he is cleaning out her flat because she us unlikely
to ever come back

never again will she be beside me
never again will we be able to show how much we can tolerate
each other
never again will the smell of her fish-head soup
boiling away for what seemed like days
waft up into my flat
until it hung in the air of every room
keep me company again

because that's exactly what it was

the neighbour from number 19

when I come out of the block
the man from number 19 is in the bin-chute again
it's the 4th time we've met this way
there's a small gas hob in there
one of those ones you'd use on a canal boat
or on the kitchen side of a bedsit
it is dirty, brown-coloured dirty
full of the spilt grease and dregs of previous use

morning, I say to him

he is shocked by my sudden appearance

oh, morning, he says back
somebody moved this down to the bins
I left it outside our door
and the council man must've thought it was to be chucked

oh, I say

I know he is lying
I can see on top of it a note that says

I WORK – PLEASE TAKE ME

plus the council don't come around in the evenings
and they certainly don't remove rubbish from outside your door
that'd be a letter job
if anything

they're useful those things, I say

he says, yes
I was planning to clean it up and use it for...

his sentence trails off
unfinished

it is colder for some than most
snow is perpetually forecast
and they need to gather up
everything that makes them feel warmer

cloud workers

they have put two black boxes on the wall next to the intercom
door of our flats

they are for the home-caterers and remote spa-workers
who if they can't get an answer from their customers
flip the lid and press in a code that opens up the doors they need
to let them in

when they get to the customer's flat
that door has already opened as well
it's all connected

technology gets a bad rep
but sometimes
after you've got over all of the jobs it's taken away
it can be a good thing
the difference between death or a continuation of the pain
Hansel and Gretel wouldn't have needed all of those white
pebbles
if they'd had Google Maps

and by the time the home-caterers and remote spa-workers enter
the customer's premises
the customer is still only half-way between their bedroom and
the front door

oh they say have you got a key then?

no they say back it's all part of the service
before explaining how it all works
for the umpteenth time

I'm not sure I like that the customer says
anyone who knows the numbers could get in
and steal or rob or even
kill me

the home-caters and remote spa-workers tut
before reassuring the customer again that their code is safe
that it's stored up in the clouds
that they don't even know it until they press the button on the app
ten minutes before the appointment is due

the home-caterers and remote-spa workers
get down to cleaning up the shit
and heating up the soup

they receive their £9.50 an hour pay in the same way
tapping 'complete' on the app once each appointment finishes
no one pays for their time in between appointments
no one compensates them for their bus or tube fares
no one speaks to them at all
reports on the state and wellbeing of the customer
are sent in via the app as well
if they get read it's not acknowledged
sometimes it's like nothing exists anymore
just gathered in this one great big cloud
to be stored

to be used one day
and not the next

the coliseum

that sits in the centre
of the circular layout of our flats
that makes up our estate
has been reclaimed

for years it had been occupied by kids
who congregated there and laughed kissed fought chased shared
clashed
grew
with other kids

Orange Park it came to be known
but we knew that wasn't its real name
that was what the Council had started the process with
for us
it was always the playground
the swings
the coliseum

it's where we all smoked our first fag
drunk our first can of beer in the open air
acting like Charlie Big Potatoes

it's where Paul
after years of mickey-taking and bullying
first got the rage and courage on
to charge at Billy Irvine
and hit him back

it's where we used to play dodgeball
had
kiss chase
champ
goal-to-goal
where we used to come

in our variations of blue green and red kits
to take sides
playing 5-asides that took on more importance
than World Cups
than FA Cup Finals

it's where Dean The Twin had his first fit
us all gathered around him
shouting out instructions
to turn him on his side
to make sure he doesn't swallow his tongue
as Tony The Twin cried
because he thought he was losing his brother

it's where Paula Smith
dared on
took a swing up to its limits
up to its threshold
where the chains loosen and everything loses its gravity a bit
before snaping tight on the way back
sending that swing sideways and up and down
with her trying to hold on

that's just kid's talk I know
astronauts go through far worse
but she was the first one to do it round our way
attempt to become an astronaut
and that lives on in me
and with us all who witnessed it I hope
her going higher up into the air
than anyone else had ever dared go before

our playground
it was an important place
like Giza like the Kaaba like Stonehenge

and now in the flat
where I used to press my nose against the windows
to see if The Twins or Paula were down there
mucking about on the slides or the swings
now there is a big white tarpaulin sheet
with City of Westminster Housing Project printed on it
and cranes are bolted into the earth where we once played
and builders come every day
to feed their families
lifting bricks up and down ladders all day
helping to construct this money-making machine
on our playground
12 units starting at £350-grand
with 4 more that have been set aside
for 'affordable housing'
to satisfy the regulators
to satisfy the particulars
each 'unit' costing one-hundred-and-seventy-five-thousand-
pounds

Ha! affordable housing for who?

as all of the playgrounds and swings
all of our coliseums
disappear
for money

Church Street market caff

for Eileen – who has suddenly been returned to the peat

I go to the counter
and ask the Irish girls

what's the special today?

the three of them
make a half circle
and all in unison
they say

boiled bacon and cabbage
or steak and kidney pud
Martin

then I go

BBC or steak an kid!
that was the special yesterday!

then they go

I know
Martin
it's the same every day

then I go

well why do you call it a special
if it's the same every day?

but by the time I've finished my sentence
they've already broken off
and are back in the kitchen
sweating over the grills
and hundreds of steaming pots

we never have
quite got the repertoire
past that

but they never get tired
of our little game
and sometimes
one of them
will shout out from the back,

because it's special bacon Martin

or

*because special people cook it for you
Martin*

and do you know what
they are most probably right

returned to the salt of the earth

in a pub still unknown to tourists and media larks
unassociated with Sky TV and £2.50 fried eggs
tucked up a side street off the Marylebone Road
under the low half-light of lamps charged with oil
pulled from the elbow-sockets of the Earth's cracked bones
this old guy
who'd fought in a war once
cleared the way with one sweep of his arm
so that he could sit down at the old Joanna
and when he got in there
he shoved his arms forwards fast enough into the air
so that the sleeves of his two-bob jacket rose up
revealing backs of hands ridged with veins
and fingers
longer than a witch's boney nose

he'd fought his whole life for a bit of this
this was his time again
as the peppermint and snuff-recovering ladies sat back in their seats
anticipating the memories this man was about to conjure back up
and let loose through their cleft network of bones
letting their top lips and tongues dip into their gin
while men with only 5-years left in 'em
prepared themselves for memories they thought
had been lost to the sea and the fog
and as we stood by the bar there
having chanced upon this wake in this battle cruiser time-warp off
the Marylebone Rd
the whole place suddenly went up
when he sent those witches bones
down onto those keys
thumping out another rendition of *'roll out the barra'*
as everyone above the age of 75
suddenly threw back their heads and belted out the words
rocking back and forth in their seats

or else jigging about on the spot
holding hands with this woman
who'd recently been returned to the salt of the earth
for just this one last time more

Brighton

I catch a train down to the seaside on a Friday afternoon
when normally I would be at work
but they give you twenty-days paid holiday a year
and you've got to use them up
somehow
even though you've got no money to do anything with them

when I get off the train
I head straight for the sea
to find the bench
I remember my mum used to take me to sit on
near the old burnt down pier
when everything was younger
and pubs used to shut in the afternoon

the air is good
and the seagulls still know how to live
gliding up on the wind like that
only coming down to stick their heads in a discarded cornet
a chip bag

it was a disaster she said
when the pier went up in flames
all of those toffee apple and candy floss machines
those goldfish and teddy bears
the huts that used to house gypsies with boney hands
that used to spread out over crystal balls
telling you your future
that you weren't very far away
from love or death
who doesn't know that anyway?

it was a disaster she said
it all going up like that
and I remember feeling sad
when she said it

but I like it better now
this charcoal black tongue sticking out into the sea
the twisted metals of the dance hall frame
pieces of iron fractured like an old woman's teeth
the legs still sturdy
charred roots pinching their toes into the seabed
just about managing
to always keep it propped up

memories live under the sea she said
they twist and turn
stretching themselves out around our submerged architectures
like nightie-wearing ghosts
and sometimes the tide breaks them free
so that they rise for attention

I go and buy myself another bottle of wine
return to our bench
to drink it
and sometimes they say
when the wind picks up off the sea
you can hear the music
that the ghosts of the girls and boys
still spin each other around to
out there
at the end of our burnt down piers

on this 11th floor scrapyard ward

there are no Buddhist's around here
just this inventory of knackered vehicles
whose engines have almost clunked to a halt
a broken stillness of defunct oil filters
clogged up with irremovable dirt
of turbos shot fuel-pipes split
spark plugs imploded exhaust systems cracked
of drive shafts
popped out of their casings
wreaking havoc now
at the abdominal wall

on this 11th floor scrapyard ward
the windows are cruelly big
as though over there the city still hums and makes gold
as if you in your last vibrations of life need to know that
the sky is also bigger in here
clouds roll and swell into clusters
whose shapes and immensity mimic
the evil thing
blooming now in your bladder

who made this world
these chemicals and amino acids
these hearts we put so much into
these whale songs and the tiger's roar
these fists of corruptible cells
that can decide to split and shadow a lung
whenever they want to

there are no Buddhist's around here
just these dying things attached to machines
that beep every time they run out of drugs
that imminent clunk again
of a broken engine
spewing out unannounced black oil
into a styrofoam dish
wheezing for the sun to set
its final black sky of silence

it will soon be over –
everything will become smaller
and nothing will ever be seen
through your eyes again

sometimes it's just hard to know what to do

I picked up my pack of bubble gum
and went to the counter to pay the man
behind it
he had on a brown and red-checked shirt
and his face was younger
than mine
he took it from my hand
picked up the scanner-gun from the desk
and began to scan the packet
with a beam of red light
we both stood there waiting for that ping
that meant the till had registered the product
and would then tell the man how much to charge me
he moved that red beam of light over the barcode
six or seven times
and neither of us heard that ping
he looked up at me
'it's not connecting,' he said
I had the 50p ready in my hand
'it's not connecting,' he said again
then he called out for someone to come and help him
and a girl came from behind me
walking over to us
but before she could say anything
the man behind the counter held up the bubble gum
and asked her if she knew what the code was for these
she turned around on her heals
and made off to where I'd picked up the bubble gum from
there were now four or five people behind me
and they were all becoming irritated
I wanted to move out of the way
let them through
because some things you try
and they just don't work
like giving up wine

working
and love
after a long minute the girl came back
with a piece of paper in her hand
and read out to the man behind the counter
what the code was
after having to check it twice the man asked me for 50p
I gave it to him
picked up my bubble gum from the counter
walked out into the open air
peeled open the wrapper
and stuck one in my ugly mouth

sometimes
it's just hard to know what to do

a forgotten friendship

I liked Lisa
she wore Levis and loved Paul Weller
every Friday she'd walk in with a bee-hive
and mini skirt on
ready for the weekend

at lunch we used to talk about the lyrics of The Kinks
I'd tell her about The Clash
she'd tell me about Joy Division
I'd tell her how much it hurt when Curtis hung himself
she told me back
that her dad did that

she turned me on to bands I'd never heard of
I brought her in tapes of The Doors Nine Below Zero The Slits
and Robert Johnson
she spat on my jeans once
I spat on hers back

she had two false teeth at the front on a plate
the originals knocked out in a Tomahawk accident before she
was big enough to ride a Chopper
she used to drop them out so that they dangled down over her
bottom lip
then pretend to be Frankenstein

she was the best telephonist in the whole gaff
150 calls a day she could take
without breaking into a sweat or even trying

she left in the end
went on maternity leave and just never returned

I never did get to tell her
that my mum 'kissed' Ray Davies in the toilets of the old
Shepherds Bush bowling alley
it wasn't like we were in love or anything
just two mates
who liked music and a laugh

it's hard to know if a friendship ever truly ends
because sometimes they come back
for a moment or two
warm you up
then just go again
leaving you unsure whether you have lost
or found something

objectification

I am in love with Jane McDonald
she has a show on the tele
she goes on cruise ships around the world
holding a cam-recorder out in front of her
on one of those extended arm thingys
and she catches her encounters with other passengers
as she drinks gin
communicates with them
before falling asleep inside her cabin

I have read Dostoevsky Camus Heaney
Bukowski Hughes and Hemingway
but none of those men
make me feel like watching Jane McDonald does

she is up for anything
she is into people
adventure
song
the sea
and laughter

she never feels down
never feels depressed
and
she is double fit

sometimes
when I'm in the shower
and I've had a little bit too much to drink
I write into the shampoo suds on the shower door
I love Jane McDonald

you can keep your Beyoncé's
your Kim Kardashian's
your Taylor Swift's
all of your supermodels
and all of your Hollywood actresses
too

just give me more
of Jane

she is the only thing
I need
to get through

the memory maker

sparkles come in many forms she said
as she pulled at my hair and stamped on my toes

she'd line up the bottles I'd drunk the night before – two beers
two wine – sometimes three wine – and she'd sparkle then as
she'd nod at their cold uselessness on the kitchen side
and then at mine

she'd sparkle every last week of the month as the money run out
pulling that hurt little pout before telling me how she never
wanted to get with a man whose only life-plan was to get
through each month still breathing still just about able to pull on
his socks
because what use does that do her!?

she'd sparkle when her OCD went wrong - when she'd drop a
Detox wipe on the floor – halfway through wiping a tin of baked
beans before it was allowed through the door – she'd stop still
then – freeze – seeing the contamination crawling all over the
floor – her in her surgeon's gloves not knowing what to do –
eventually sparkling like a river pouring off the edge of a
mountain for hours

and when she panic-attacked she'd sparkle all over the place until
the broken glass fell from her eyes throwing words around like
they weren't really knives asking me to leave as I was suffocating
her and she couldn't breathe wanting me out of her sight so she
could stop sparkling
and calm down

but the best sparkles were the Friday nights just after I got paid
when she'd tell me to turn the music up and dance with me
around the front room with glitter falling out of her ears and
stars circling her head drinking wine with me holding my hand
to help her draw out her plan for the next month's money
before pulling me into the bedroom
where she'd sparkle like a jewel sewn into the gown of our bed
where she'd make another one
and stab it in through the back of my head

a critical analysis from a bored wife on holiday

look at the sky she said
it is bigger than all of your poems
put together

look at that tree she said
it has more life in it
than all of your poems
put together

look at the sea she said
it is deeper than all of your poems
put together

look at that dog shit
on the promenade
that somebody hasn't bothered
to clean up
that
is one of your poems

it was a hot day
we were on holiday
hand in hand
walking by the sea
and everything
was just how it should be

through the screams and the fire

the hardest thing to do
is live with all of the misplaced rage

the controllers
raging about the immigrants taking over
the boys on speed in the bar
raging about the diving in football
the fat-cats in waistcoats
raging about tax
the daughter raging about money
the son raging about honey
her
31-years in and still
the rage over the light not being turned out in the bathroom
the rage of the larder door being left open
the rage of socks left on the floor
the rage of a wine-spill on the bathroom floor

there were people dying in Syria
and Northampton
the NHS was on its knees
footballers were earning 300-grand-a-week
and all of the greats
were dead
but my wine-spill
was the only thing
that'd get her excited

and boy did she give it me

how the fuck do you get wine
on the bathroom floor
what is wine even doing
in the bathroom
anyway?

I didn't have an answer

so I decided to buy her a rose
brought it home on its own
apart from a bottle of wine
and in the lift
I said to that rose

you're gonna do it for me tonight flower
your beauty
stuck on the end of this stem
it's gonna work
I'm gonna hand you over to her
and you're gonna whisper into her ear
that she needs to take the back of my head in her hands
and kiss me again
tell me how much she loves me
I'm counting on you flower
we are in this together!

and then I pressed my nose into it
and the smell and its velvety softness
made me think that everything
was gonna be ok

but when I went in
she was already waiting for me
just behind the door
screaming at me
telling me how she'd been waiting for me to come home
so she could tell me what an idiot I am
because when I went to work I'd left the front door open
and a man from the energy company had peered in
asking if he could read the meter
catching her naked in the hall
apart from a pair of black knickers

I screwed the rose up
and chucked it outside
then I started hitting myself in the face
hoping it'd make her stop

but it didn't
and I didn't have the guts
to keep on hurting myself
in the hope that she would stop

so I just walked in
through the screams and the fire
opened up the wine
and began sipping at it
wishing that I was in Syria

dads don't know everything they just pretend to

when my son asks me if England are going to win the World
Cup
I tell him
of course they are

when my son asks me if he can see
the next Star Wars film at the Imax when it comes out
I tell him
of course we can

when my daughter asks me
why I only ever seem to wear the same four shirts to work
over and over every week
I tell her that it is a magic trick
that if anyone found out that I actually wore more
then the whole world would end
and no one would be able to eat any ice cream anymore

when she asks me
if one day I will buy her a ticket to fly off to Cuba
so she can dance laced with sweat in a basement Havana club
wearing a red silk dress
pressed up tight against a man who's uncle once stubbed out the
butts of sucked down cigars
on the face of an American flag
I tell her
no worries
we'll make that happen hun

and when the boy asks me
what is going to happen to him when I die
where he'll live
if he will inherit my council tenancy agreement
that I keep banging on about being under threat
I tell him
not to worry
because his dad is never going to die
and that all of the wolves have dentist insurance
so it doesn't matter what happens to their teeth
and that the stars
are not really balls of fire
that most probably are dead cold holes by now
that the real reason for them
why they keep blinking on and off
up there in the sky like that
is because they are the eyes of his dead nan
amazed at how much he is growing

I know
I'm a shit dad
I should be preparing them differently
but the working world is a far shittier place
and one day
it's going to break them both in two
like it has done
to me and you

Alexander the Great before the walls of Tyre

you could tell that the new supervisor
wanted us to start thinking very quickly
that he was someone to be feared
by the way he ripped into Faye on his first morning
for being 10-minutes late back from her break
when any new supervisor worth his salt
would've done his homework first
learnt that Faye was a woman who worked her fingers to the
bone
and needed to be cultivated kept on side
because she was always the first one with her arm up
whenever a weekend shift needed covering

and the way he stood over you
as you were controlling away
his hands clasped behind his back
as though he was taking in every movement and allocation
looking for an error he was there to correct
when in reality it was all just a blur to him
which he'd given up trying to follow within the first five seconds
of him standing there
trying to do his supervising

and then there were the questions he was asked by the
telephonists
about times for couriers
why they were late
that he deferred and pointed towards one of us controllers
while giving them this faraway look
as though he was an admiral on the bridge
staring off at something no one else could see
before nosing his head at it
pretending to be taking down
a mental note of great importance

and then there was the way
he started getting us all to hush
just before the 10 o'clock rush every morning
so that he could deliver a fire and brimstone speech
designed to put the fear of the Antichrist up us
so that we all knew how much was at stake
that we needed to remain sharp and focused
'idiot-mistakes' free
but which only made the older controllers
crack up on the insides
like who does he think he is man?
Alexander the Great before the walls of Tyre?
and all of the less experienced controllers
to retract into their shells
too frightened to take on any responsibility
or make any decisions
so that we all walked out into that control room
in various states of fear hilarity terror and confusion

if anything about our previous supervisors was to go by
he was going to make it this one
right to the top

the men with no guts

sit in aeroplanes in seats bigger than the sun
sipping at cocktails thousands of miles above the Earth
the men with no guts send emails to share information
that they should be sharing face to face
if only they had the guts

the men with no guts have little black books
with lists of all the men they consider superfluous to
requirements
who they wouldn't mind seeing split apart
sat in a shop doorway somewhere
or forced to queue in a foodbank

the men with no guts can't sing or feel a song like a controller can
like a mechanic a construction worker a fireman or an auxiliary
nurse can
the men with no guts wrench their songs up out of their throats
with pulleys equations and the clank of steel
rather than letting them rise
slowly up from rib to rib
until they enter throats and float out of mouths
that need those songs more than the air they breathe

the men with no guts don't get up at 5am every morning
to go in and grind out 55-hour-weeks
so that they can hold onto a job between their teeth
like a dog
the men with no guts get up at 7am
stop off at fancy coffee shops on their way in
sit in chairs for less than 8-hours a day
staring into spreadsheets that they maneuver and manipulate
so that they can protect their jobs
and place others in jeopardy

the men with no guts holiday in Thailand twice a year they drink
£50 bottles of Pinot Noir they pay
for dwarves to step into dinosaur costumes for their kids'
birthday parties moan
about the service when their £200 dinners are served 8-minutes
late create
when everything doesn't go as smoothly
as their wealth deserves it to go

the men with no guts
turn everything into plastic
so that they can better mould bend then snap it
while all of those who still have some left
find themselves walking around their flats naked in the early
hours of the morning
unable to sleep
wondering why
they feel like they are the only ones left

man management

Davy has not been the same since the supervisors sat Emmanuel
down next to him as his new right-hand man and told them
both to learn to work together

there were differences between them that they couldn't resolve
when Emmanuel wasn't sitting next to Davy
so how the supervisors came up with the idea that sitting them
next to each other would resolve it
is something only stars know

Davy wants to know why Emmanuel bites his nails
Emmanuel wants to know why Davy has a tattoo of a lion on his
left forearm
Davy asks Emmanuel why he keeps running his hands through
his hair
Emmanuel asks Davy why he keeps sniffing all the time
if it's because he has a constant cold or
something else is going on

the rest of us controllers
can feel it all brewing
feel it rising
until on Friday 3rd March at 1.30pm
with all of the jobs dropping down on the screen
and the supervisors circling about
Emmanuel asks Davy why 'our screen
seems to be the only one full of so many uncovered jobs
when all the other controllers' screens
seem to be under control'
causing Davy to snap stand up
and push Emmanuel at both shoulders
with enough force so that his controller's chair toppled over
backwards and down
with Emmanuel's legs dangling about up in the air

before Emmanuel could roll over and get up to have a go back at
Davy
the supervisors were there
holding the two of them back

as the rest of us controllers all looked up into the false ceiling
wondering how many more times will they pit us together
just to see what happens

the list inside his little black book

there was a rumour that it existed
but no one had ever seen it

some people swore they had caught a glimpse of it
every time he finished off one of his grand-plan theory talks
and then smirked that charming smile of his
like you were both now in on it

others said that it had to exist
because there were just too many good people
who'd been thrown off the boat
two-hundred-miles out at sea

others spoke in hushed tones about it
as if the fact of just being heard
talking about it
meant that you might get put on it

there were the ones you knew had their ears open for him
but worse were the ones who didn't even plan
to tell him this or that
but found themselves sitting in front of him
in that 5th floor office of his
spilling the beans
in the hope that this would gain them
some kind of immunity from it

but no matter how much you tried
no matter how much you just got your head down
grinding out those 11-hour shifts
you never really knew where it was
or how it crept
all you could feel was what must've been its hot breath
on the back your neck

and then BOOM!

another one chucked over the side
two-hundred-miles out at sea

and then BOOM!

another one *managed out of the business*

and then BOOM!

another one who had to go home
to tell their woman that they'd lost their job
or that they were being transferred
to the Slough office
or that from the start of next month
they were being made to go on night shifts
with no clear reason of why
of what they had done
other than the rumours
that they were on the list inside his little black book
and nothing now
could be done about it

what the loss of revenue feels like

'I don't have all the answers' head supervisor Harry tells us
controllers
who have all been gathered in his office
after the loss of a big account
'but I sure as hell know the problems'

then he took his glasses off
and started turning his head slowly around the room
making sure his eyes met each pair of ours
so that he could let us know
that he was looking at all of us

us
who have to work on an operating system
that it is so high-tech and temperamental
not even the guys from IT know how to fix it us
who have to work with couriers who don't even know where
Soho is
who get taken on just because they have a valid passport a satnav
and are willing to drive through the streets at ridiculous speeds
for loose change us
who are in the third year of a pay freeze
despite the electricity going up the water rates going up
fish milk Marmite meat us!
who have had our lunch breaks reduced
from sixty-minutes to thirty
so that our shifts have become thirty-minutes longer
without any monetary recompense us!
who go home after those shifts and medicate ourselves
with skunk wine Diazepam
plugging ourselves into Instagram Facebook Netflix
just so we can escape it all
cage it all up for moments us!
sheered of any opportunity or voice
to challenge the assumption

that we have been given an operating system and resource
that is adequate
one which will keep us all safe from disaster
safe from the monster's jaws
US!
all gathered there
in head supervisor Harry's office
getting told that we are the problem
why the company has lost
another big account

'and do you know what?
what the directors are going to say about this?
that the only way you lot are going to actually get it
to actually learn
what the loss of revenue feels like
is to let one of you go'

we filed out
back into the control room
to take up our seats and put on our headsets
to begin trying again
to work out what the operating system was trying to tell us
trying to explain to one of our couriers
exactly where Fleet Street is
all the while wondering who was going to be the one
the one Harry was on about
the one who was going to be laid off
have to go home to tell his wife
that he's lost his job
lost his income
because all of the conditions and rules and procedures
were considered sound and solid enough
so that whenever anything went wrong
what other answer could there be
other than it was all our fault
that one of us was going to have to go
if nothing else to teach us about suffering

if nothing else to teach us about loss
if nothing else
to equalise the pain
now being felt inside those shareholders'
spreadsheet hearts

nothing left to dream about anymore

Edward made the decision
to give up his pursuit of a job in economics
that he'd spent 3-years getting a degree for
to come and work in our control room
as a right-hand man
because he couldn't afford
to work for another 6-months with no pay
just to get a stamp and a tick on his CV

Magic Mike made the decision
to abandon his dream
of becoming a Formula 1 mechanic
and took up a role in our workshop
resuscitating almost dead bikes
so that we could get another 10,000 miles out of them
before they died
not because he didn't have the skill in his fingertips
and that instinct in his guts
that could diagnose an engine's problems
merely by the sound of its revs
but because he just didn't know enough people
with the right keys
to open up the right doors

Grace made the decision
to accept the promotion offered her
from part-time telephonist to new telephonist supervisor
giving up on her dream
of running her own fashion empire
from out of her flat
because 'a little bit of profit' wasn't enough anymore
to fund a dream
when you've got two teenagers to support

and a man who's left you to go and live in Blackpool
to try and realise his dream
of becoming a slag
and a nightclub crooner

Paul made the decision
to apply to an ad on Gumtree
looking for a recruitment clerk
to work in a courier company
giving up on his dream
of becoming the head chef of a Michelin starred restaurant
and now sits in the basement under me
interviewing applicant after applicant
trying to fill these vans of ours
with other men
who also haven't got anything left
to dream about anymore either

but there is one man
in this building
who has realised his dream
who has a Bentley parked in the yard outside
to prove it
who sits in the boardroom upstairs
working out what decisions
he can get away with
what human being he can lay off next
what outsourcing company
he can replace the cleaners with
how he can swap
someone's shifts around
so that he can make that someone work
one weekend a month instead
and save even more
on overtime
add another fifth of a percent
to the bottom line
making his dream

become a little bit richer
a little bit more
vivid
a little bit
more
speckled with blood

when the new guy takes over

the new guy brought in to head up sales and make things happen
wears a black shirt tight against his gym-trimmed body
he is a Vegan believes in Lucifer
he walks around the control room like a sniper
picking off things here and there
storing them all up in his mind
ready to raise them back up out of the soil in meetings
as a reference to why everything is going wrong
and he is now here to fix it

the new guy brought in to head up sales and make things happen
lives in Highgate
he drives a car bigger than Ronnie's bedsit
he doesn't drink coffee he doesn't drink wine he doesn't know life
but he does know Excel
how to manipulate it so that he looks like a magician
a magic-man their saviour
he is the new religion
cool and smelling of cash-rich ideas
that will eventually do away with some of our wages

the new guy brought in to head up sales and make things happen
has a woman back home barricaded in the bathroom
screaming out for love
refusing to come out until she gets it
screaming for intimacy
screaming for cuddles
screaming for a man to fuck her back to life again
sail her back out into the Universe-black
where stars explode and no one truly understands yet
why dead hearts come back from merely being warmed up again

the new guy brought in to head up sales and make things happen
has an office with big glass doors
he sits in it
behind its desk shuffling papers around like a Nazi
comes out every now and then to assassinate us
stick a gold star on our sleeves
turn his nose up at the air we breathe

when we all go home after our shifts
we have to pass it
those big glass doors
and we spit on them
leave trails of our gob on his door

but he doesn't see us do it
he has already gone home
back to his cold existence
where he'll sit in his study ignoring her screams
plotting the next strike
of his takeover

Gorbachev's land

Gorbachev, the company cat
who has a red splodge of fur
that drips from his forehead down over his right eye
is the CEO of the workshop's backyard
nothing here threatens him
he is the Last King of Scotland here
as he spreads himself out in the sun
sprawled over the griddle-hot bonnet on one of our vans
that are all parked in a row
awaiting new couriers to jump in them
to see if they can earn a living

Gorbachev couldn't give a toss though
he is drunk on the blood of rats
just about managing to get up
before lazily sauntering the whole length of the yard atop the
roofs of those vans
like he is an Emperor
in his ginger-white robes
licked clean of the blood he spilled the night before
the only rat and mouse free area
along the whole stretch of dirty canal
that slinks along behind this workshop away into Harlesden

Gorbachev
who if he can't be found on top of one of those vans
letting his subjects see his lack of fear
see how he licks his balls
then would be under one of them
checking that nothing is festering
or gaining hold in his sewers
slinking under the whole row of vans
checking behind every wheel
every nut and bolt
until he comes to the bins at the end of the yard and sniffs

instantly taking in every square-inch
before turning around on his spine
and heading back again

Gorbachev the company cat
is Emperor
the Commander in Chief
the Fuhrer and CEO of this yard
he meets out his will with impunity
nothing here threatens him

unlike the mechanics and controllers
who eat their lunches on the benches opposite Gorbachev's row
of vans
watching Gorbachev
like he is a reality TV star
watching him in awe
like guests in his palace
admiring his calm grace that they once had
when they were young and fearless
admiring his disdain as they call out to him,
'Oi! Gorbachev! you handsome fella,
you killed any rats lately?'

the mechanics and controllers
who are never quite sure what their CEO
is going to come up with next
but sure as hell know
that whatever it is
it won't be anywhere near as swift or fair
as it is for the subjects
in Gorbachev's land

going for lunch with Ronnie

when Ronnie's lunch break coincides with mine
we go to Sainsbury's together
and I know as we are trying to cross the Whitechapel Rd
dodging the cars and the vans
that something will happen
something always happens when you are with Ronnie
it is what makes him one of the greats
but yesterday it started early
before we'd even got in the shop
when a man wearing a brown cotton suit
offered him a leaflet
Ronnie taking it and stopping to read it
me off still thinking I was talking to him about the food we were
about to eat
turning around when I heard the commotion
seeing Ronnie shouting at him

so you're saying there's this fella
who can sort it all out for me
give me freedom from my sins
freedom from my skin
freedom from this?

Ronnie lifting up his t-shirt
and showing him his fat belly
pointing at it
me knowing that he needed me
so I went back and grabbed his arm
telling him that we were on lunch
needed food
as he reluctantly stopped
and let me push him into Sainsbury's
but I could tell he was on the verge
of having one of his turns
and when we got in the noodle pot isle

he took ten-minutes running his hands through his hair
bending down and picking up pots
reading the contents placing them back
humming and haring
telling me where this pot was made
what that pot contained
before picking up the same one he always does
Itsukatsu curry flavour
me with my six chicken wings getting cold in a bag
thinking we're off now to pay
but Ronnie stopping in the veg aisle wanting beetroot
telling me that the little balls of them drowned in vinegar

that's not beetroot man
these are!

diving in to pick up the vacuum-packed ones

no vinegar you see
just beetroot in their natural juices

flinging them all over the place
trying to find the right sizes and shapes that made Ronnie's
world turn right
the Sainsbury's man coming over to ask me
if everything was alright
me winking a yes at him
Ronnie super aware saying to himself

no, it's not alright!

bent over digging in amongst the black totes
until he found the right pack
right at the back of of them all
holding them up to the light saying

these are the ones I want
beautiful
perfect buds ripped out of the earth
sealed goodness

us then both going off to pay
me hoping the whole time
that the Jehovah's Witness man had gone
but as we walked out I saw he was still there
so I got myself in between him and Ronnie's route
Ronnie trying to get back around behind me
so he could pass him by face to face
me like a collie dog dropping back and herding him away
Ronnie shouting

idiot!

over my shoulder
as I got him back across the Whitechapel Rd
and back into work

Ronnie saying in the silence of the lift
as we went up to our floor

sorry mate
I know I'm a handful sometimes
but this life man
the people
and all of the stuff
it just makes me so...so...
I don't know
me nodding an it's okay at him
walking out the lift
and back into that control room
wondering the whole time
what it must be like to be the owner of a mind
capable of detonating at any minute

Ronnie's guts on show

sometimes
in Summer
when all of the world was singing
and the sky was that blue colour
that made you feel like you were on holiday
Ronnie used to come in totally relaxed

he used to bring that 22-stone frame of his in
and sit it down next to you
making you feel like you were not sitting next to a nuclear bomb
and he'd look you in the eyes and smile
wink even
ask you how you were doing
totally ignorant of the power he had in him
and it was almost like Ronnie was normal
that he had a home kids and a dog
eat pasta of a night for dinner
kicked his shoes off after a long day at work
and supped on a beer while watching the tele
just like the rest of us

but we knew it wouldn't last for long
we knew that Ronnie had his own weather patterns swirling
around
that it didn't matter whether it was Summer or Winter
because anything was possible up there
and that sometime soon
he would erupt again
spill himself out
not caring about the rules and procedures
make a big scene about him maybe being proper mental
that all of this trying to be able to get on
with this working and controlling lark
trying to fit in
was pointless
because

maybe I am just destined to have to be contained
feel like an imposter
continually feeling like I am coated in this weird electricity

and when he got that in his head
Ronnie used to get up and start stalking around the control
room
holding his head in his hands
refusing to sit down in his chair
as we all tried to herd him up like a wild pig
before the supervisors clocked on
sit him down and slap him around the face
knock him out of this madness that sometimes descended on
him
get him back down to allocating out the jobs
as though nothing had happened

him later in the pub
disappearing into a sink-hole of guilt
telling us all how much he loves us
respects us
for looking after him like that
us
half-drunk on beer and tequila
telling him to shut up
secretly wishing that we had only half the guts
he was prepared to show

shining through the mud

in between the stop-still-suddenly
staring-up-at-the-ceiling silences
that caused everybody within a two-room radius
to feel on edge feel
the electricity that Ronnie could generate
crackle through the air

in between the panic attacks
that made him abandon any pretense
that he was making headway
at being able to function properly
inside a control room
which caused him sometimes
to have to suddenly get up from his controller's chair
and announce to his fellow controllers
that he thinks he is having one of his turns
might just need to go outside
so that he can deep breath
and calm down

in between those moments
where Ronnie couldn't help
but openly show
the hurt that's been done him
by the system
the scars left behind
by his mum and dad
by his doctors
who thought nothing of ploughing him full of drugs
by his social workers
who only sat there and spoke to him
so that they could tick boxes
and put crosses next to his name

in between all of that
Ronnie lives
a mountain of a man
with four failed suicide attempts and an on and off Tramadol
addiction going on
with eyes bigger and brighter than a sun
a heart that could sometimes
spread its warmth out like an explosion
warming up the loneliest places on Earth
with its generosity and self-depreciating wit
that could often make everybody within its explosion's radius
feel that this world wasn't as cold and lonely
as first thought
that we weren't actually
anywhere near going to have to give up yet
and most probably never would
while people like Ronnie were still around
prepared to let us see them
trying to shine through the mud

Jamie Oliver might as well live on another fucking planet

when we walked through the door
after 11-hours working at those control screens
and 2-hours back and forth
on the tube
we kicked our boots off and collapsed
onto a couch or into a chair
with a kebab and a can of beer in our hands
with a box of fried chicken and wine beside us –
a grab-bag of Munchies for afters

I don't think I knew any one of us
who went home to stand around for an hour
boiling vegetables and poaching chicken breasts
stirring a pot of stew
as it simmered it's smells and goodness
throughout the tiny spaces we lived in

we were just too knackered too empty
lots of what had been inside us
like energy and will and self-esteem
had been evaporated by the day –
the monotony the anxiety
steaming it all away –
and the regulation of dietary habits
was just one more impossible hurdle
to face

so we gave in
to the chicken shops the kebab shops
the fat and the grease
anything that brought us
a bit of comfort and peace

later
crisps Pepperami's and ice cream
would be taken on the bed
watching the foodies on the tele
fetishising over the intricacy of food
made with expensive ingredients
that we couldn't afford
or even if we could
muster up the energy or will
to cook

and as Ronnie used to say
when discussing his insatiable appetite and 22-stone frame

Jamie Oliver might as well live
on another fucking planet
as far as I'm concerned

what might live on the other side of the moon

Jamie has started working harder than usual
he has started coming in for work 20-minutes early
making a big noise about cleaning down his workstation
so that everyone could see and hear
that Jamie is coming in for work 20-minutes early

he is now making sure that his fleet attendance forms
are filled in by the 11 o'clock deadline
when before they used to lay around his desk
with crumbs from bacon sandwiches and coffee cup rings all
over them

he is actually talking to customers and colleagues now
engaging witty sympathetic
looking people in the eye and smiling
when before he used to hide away from everything
swerve any intimacy or confrontation
getting up to go to the toilet whenever he sensed a 'situation'
developing

his fingers float along his keyboard now
when before they used to just about manage to rise
before dropping down like wrecking balls onto those keys
his eyes his demeanor his breathing
everything about him is lighter now
more in sync
as he tells us across the table we eat our lunches on
that he's met a new girl with flaming red hair and a tongue
that can lick life up out of the sky and hold stars in the back of
her throat
before throwing them back out again
like things shot from a catapult piercing his chest
who reads literature out to him after they've had sex
who is a vegan and who has got him eating lentils and fruit
lots and lots of fruit

who he holds hands with on walks through the park
talking about the birds and the sea what before
he thought must live on the other side of the moon
never once about work
the supervisors the couriers
who used to drive him down into corners
who used to hammer him into the floor
who used to make him feel constantly trapped
as he finishes off his 4th apple
adding as he gets up to go back into work
that also
he hasn't once thought about killing himself
in a whole month

Health and Safety check

the Health and Safety officer
sent in by the holding company
to check that its subsidiary is adhering to the rules
wears an old pin-striped suit and
has his hair in a comb-over
he is perfectly shaven
in that worn-down-skin red raw way
and he smells of soap

he walks around on his first few days
with a clipboard and pen in his hands
noting down the potential risks
to the business
that he's been brought in to mitigate

we ask to see his list

4 plug sockets hanging from walls in control room all in use and
powering computers –
landmines waiting to be trodden on
carpet come away from floor at top of staircase leading down to
main doors –
broken-neck-trap
hole in roof above control-point B with signs of mould on wall
directly underneath –
like a sad and tired old flat
no fire extinguisher in kitchen no fire extinguisher in telephonist
room and no fire extinguisher in staff lunchroom –
but no signs yet from any of the staff of fire
no toilet brushes or soap in the two dispensers of gents' toilet –
germs everywhere make note not to shake anyone's hands
fungi growing between sodden carpet recoiled from skirting board
in recruitment office
under mould-flecked wall –
like something you'd find in an abandoned estate where 30 dogs

have spent 30-years defecating and rolling about in each other's
mess
bare electric wires fanning out of open socket on accounts
department wall –
like the tentacles of an alien ready to zap you
mouse droppings in draw of abandoned desk in unused utility
room –
Chernobyl Syndrome evident
fire door not fire door but a light chipboard affair –
ready to go up like tissue when touched by flames

despite his sense of humour
it was going to be a mighty to-do list
that was for sure
and it was well noted by some of the controllers
that someone in this building
had better start packing up their stuff soon
and start looking for another job
because somebody was going to have to pay for the repairs
and it was unlikely to be the bottom line

a hole the size of a Romanian mechanic

it wasn't an old building
more neglected
with overflowing bins mould
damp on the walls
that made the air feel constantly cold

the carpet had shrunk away from the skirting board
pinched away by that damp
and when it rained
the water would leak in from above
the doors
the windows
and in through the roof
at eight separate places

and when that happened
the supervisors would suddenly appear by the cleaner's
cupboard
holding up those eight big yellow cement-buckets that the
management had bought
for just these occasions
the supervisors yelling out
'bucket time boys, it's bucket time, come and get your buckets'
and then we'd all jump up from our seats
to take those buckets from their hands
before rushing around placing them under the fountains of rain
that were now pouring down into our control room
like a series of waterfalls flicked on by a switch
in an amusement park

we knew something more efficient needed to be done
when the mushrooms started to come
punching their velvet fists through the floor's wet weak-spots
in between the carpet and skirting
appearing almost overnight glistening
on the first charge of their takeover

the roofers were too expensive
it was said
so they sent one of the mechanics up there
to try and fill the holes
but we didn't know that
until halfway through eating our lunch
when he came crashing through the roof
his legs appearing through the ceiling first
running away like a Bolt in midair
before it all suddenly gave way
and the rest of him came
the false ceiling frame finally giving in
bent from the heat
of him now coming through at a million-miles-an-hour
freeing the trapped water and dust
all over the place
as it caught up with him and drenched his head
leaving a hole behind him
the size of a Romanian mechanic
and him on the floor
clutching his leg

we all gathered around him to see if he was alright
bending in
turning our heads up peering up through that ceiling and roof
up through that hole
that let in the bluest sky we'd ever seen seagulls
circling around up there
so far away they looked like prayer flags fluttering about in the
wind
then back down at him
all of us wondering
what the hell was going to be allowed
to happen next

accidents in the gig-economy

it's not like he needed this
not with all what he had to pay for
who relied on him

the leg was obviously broken
there was bone sticking out
shin had been snapped in two
poking there out of the skin
blood wouldn't stop coming

it wasn't the pain he minded
all he could think about was the why
why did that pedestrian step out like that
just up ahead of him enough
so that he had time to swerve
straight in front of that car
whose metal had shattered his shin
why
why couldn't it have been
two seconds later
then he wouldn't even have had time to brake
the pedestrian would've taken the full force
cushioning him
but at least he wouldn't be laying
in the middle of the road now
with his shin broken in two
not looking like he'll be able to work
for months

it's not like he needed this
not with all what he had to pay for
who relied on him
he'd worked hard to get his four jobs
crawled all over everyone
got his head down

cleaner courier security guard
food delivery at weekends
18-hours a day they took up

cleaner 4am to 7am
courier 8am to 6pm
security guard 10pm to 2am
weekend food delivery midday to midnight

and now
laying in the middle of this road
with his shin bone shattered and bone sticking out
they're all as good as gone

he didn't need this
not with all what he had to pay for
who relied on him

he'd seen it happen to Kleberson
£650 a week blood couriering
then a car clipped him along with the bike
as he was standing by in Gt Portland Street
left him with a broken hip
and no way to earn any money for months
no insurance self-employed gig-economy
may as well have been invisible
car sped off round corner
an Uber it was a witness said
we all end up doing it to each other
there's nothing else left
to feed on or manipulate

he didn't need this
not with all what he had to pay for
who relied on him

mother mother
rent is paid for 3 more weeks mother
electricity and food?
enough for 3 more weeks mother
she's due in 3 weeks mother
the motorbike is a write off mother
I don't know mother
it's not the pain mother
it's all these zero options I have

sister sister
sorry, but I won't be able to help
towards Zico's medicine anymore
or the loan you took out
to pay back the loan you took out
when I can work again
I will help again

father father
remember when I was 9
how you sat me up on that bike and made me turn my wrist
so that I shot off down the dirt-track behind our house
all the while you shouting
'momentum is balance momentum is balance'
well I don't know if you're looking down on me now father
laying in this road with my shin snapped in two
but if you are
you couldn't help me now
could you father?

he didn't need this
not with all what he had to pay for
who relied on him

sometimes
it's all about the margins
or a matter of seconds
this surviving lark

all of the battles

Alpha Seven-Four-Nine doesn't want to do the job from Coutts
on The Strand
to Lloyd's in Southend
he lives in Egham and getting allocated that
at 4 o'clock in the afternoon
means he won't get home till gone 9

Robbie, the controller who allocated him the job, and all the
thousands of other jobs
that has enabled Alpha Seven-Four-Nine to earn over £800 a
week couriering
is incensed by his refusal

he has pushed the job over twenty times down to his app
but Alpha Seven-Four-Nine is not accepting it

a supervisor comes out and asks Robbie
why the job hasn't been covered yet
Robbie tells him that he's on it

now that the job is on their radar
Robbie knows that he's got to do something about it
or else he'll get the blame and his head ripped off
if something goes wrong

so Robbie gets Alpha Seven-Four-Nine on the phone
and tells him that he has to do it
because there is no one else

it happens sometimes

I can hear Robbie on the phone to him
telling him he's got to do it
that it's for one of the big banks
and even though it is a dog of a job
he needs to remember
that he's sorted him out hundreds of times before
and will do so again
in the future

Alpha Seven-Four-Nine knows this is true but is not going to let
Robbie get off that easily
so he goes straight in for the heart strings
talks about his kids
how if he does this job then he'll not get home in time to read
them a bedtime story
how his wife will kill him if he isn't in to help her with
everything

Robbie tells him that he needs to tell her to think about the
money
that when you take the big picture into account
he gets sorted
and that he'll remember this tomorrow if he does it
and the next day

but Alpha Seven-Four-Nine is having none of it
he doesn't want to go to Southend
he wants Robbie to beg him

this goes on for over fifteen-minutes and the job is just getting
older and older
so Robbie, because there is no one else, has no alternative but to
beg

Alpha Seven-Four-Nine still isn't doing it though
begging isn't enough sometimes

so Robbie has no alternative other than to get the big gun out
and tell Alpha Seven-Four-Nine that if he doesn't do it
then he needs to bring his company bike in
and go and find another company to work for
before putting the phone down on him

three-minutes later Alpha Seven-Four-Nine accepts the job

and all of the battles will continue again tomorrow

handover from the night shift

Quite night last night. Just one incident to report regarding Yankee 156 who called up at 1.30am to advise that he was riding along yesterday evening with a Harrods delivery on board trying to find a house down in a lane somewhere near Cobham when he happened to have a panic attack. His heart was beating fast and he thought he was going to have cardiac arrest. He then proceeded to pass out and fall from the bike while riding along. When he came too he then crawled to a person's house to knock and ask for an ambulance.

Understandably he was not able to make us aware of this at the time. He is having tests in the hospital currently and says the food is awful. I have informed Harrods that the status of their job is unknown due to the courier having a panic attack and nearly dying. They are not happy because it is a £400 silk slip for a VIP client but understand that sometimes things do not always go according to plan. Edward from Harrods Personal Shopping would like a call back in the morning to discuss how we are going to 'compensate' them for their customer's bad experience. Yankee 156 is not answering his phone anymore so I'm not sure exactly where the £400 silk slip is.

something close to magic

Babafemi has only been a courier for four weeks
but already he is learning how it can
suck the colour from your cheeks
make you think
that there's a conspiracy going on
to keep you below the waterline
pushed down in amongst the mud

there's the PCN and CCTV fines he tells me
they just appear on your payslip
in red-print deductions
not having remembered or seen
where any of them came from

those cameras are like snipers I tell him
they pick you off every time you park your van
or stay still for a moment

there's the controllers also he says
they have their own ideas of fairness
what criteria should be considered
in the allocation process
often sending him to Essex
an hour before his shift finishes
when he lives in Middlesex

and he can't moan back at them
he can't get on the phone and tell them how unfair that is
because they just say they've got work to cover
that they've got a supervisor telling them what to do too
and anyway
it's within your shift
so get on with it

then there's the pay he says

£241 I took home last week
before fuel
I know I only have one roof
but I've got three kids and a wife who live under it

I don't know what to do
nothing is getting me out of the mud

I'm not stupid
they think I am a dumb African man
who will just put up with it
but I can't anymore

last reports were the GPS had Babafemi's van in a field
somewhere near Cranbrook in Kent
at 9.30pm on a Friday night
the garbled message of his last call to the office
was that his van had run out of fuel
and that he thought there were aliens following him
before his phone run out of credit
and went dead

he will rise again somewhere
Babafemi
in another place

I don't know how they do it

this surviving lark
it is something close
to magic

Afghan Ali – courier call sign
CH Four-Three-Eight

he lays flatbreads over a bare gas flame in a shared kitchen
above a Spar in Walthamstow
filling them with dreams that their mother used to fill them
with better
before she lost her head to the Aegean Sea
his son makes weird noises in his sleep which he puts down to
being lost
but if you ask the son he'll tell you that it's because he stays
awake in his sleep
tying torches to trees
so that he can better help guide the American drones away
from his street
she goes to school in a flock of hijabs
to learn about mathematics and physics
how if you split an atom apart it can release so much energy it
can melt skin
no matter what colour it is
or how strong the bones are underneath
in home economics she learns about waste
how it needs to be recycled
rather than put in landfill or tipped into the sea
like her mother was
before he logs on to courier for us at 8 he cleans toilets
between 4 and 6 am
for a company whose owner puts £600,000 a year into the
pockets of a network that spends our tax money developing
systems that can let a bomb drop from two thousand feet
right on top of his grandmother's head
just so he can get a tax break
she carves cat flaps out of her arm
because she's been told so often how ugly the colour of her
needy blood is
that she's started believing it
and wants to let all of that animal out of her

there were only three of them left
when once there were four
and scores of others they could name
before there were even trees
their mother used to call out to from the kitchen window
but all of their leaves are gone now too
I don't know
but I can imagine only the bare arms of those trees are left
for them to hold onto

Ali used to drive for Uber but when the pandemic hit the need for drivers dropped through the floor. A mate of his who was doing work picking up test-kits from care homes gave him my number. He called me one day back in June or July of last year and asked for a job. We got him signed up and we both hit it off – soon after that we started speaking on a daily basis – he speaks to me about his shit and I tell him about my shit – he is always worried about his children – I am always worried about my job – we both want them to be safe but realise that they are, ultimately, outside of our control.

We have worked together now on this covid shit for over a year – he used to call me Mr Boss but as we have got to know each other over the year he has plugged in to my winceing and cringing about things like that – he now calls me Mr White Man Boss – and now I call him, rather than Ali, Afghan Ali – we take the piss out of each other – he tells me he thinks that I have a small dick because anyone so wrapped up in their work doing so many hours as I do can't be doing it in the bedroom 'for the lady' – I offer to show it him – he says I'm gay – that back where he comes from men like me get decapitated in sports arenas – I tell him back that where I come from men like him get shit put through their letterbox and slogans spray-painted on their doors – he says back – fuck, you think I don't know that Mr White Man Boss – I live in Walthamstow, above a Spar!

He doesn't have a wife because she drowned in the Dardanelles Straits when they were trying to get away from Afghanistan and had got that far that they were 'this far' from leaping away from Turkey into Greece and then it'd be easier then to get through into

Europe – 'but then that happened' he says, 'I held the two kids' heads up above the water but didn't have any left over for hers…' It's almost impossible sometimes, to deliver a poem about a life lived like Ali's - so what do you do? Do you write the poem or do nothing about it…do you do nothing and let none of it be said? Or do you attempt this…

where are the working class now

imagine if all of the workers in this city were white

imagine that

imagine
the Uber driving Somalian cabbie
white

the Filipino nanny
white

the Colombian cleaner
white

the Brazilian courier
white

imagine
that

imagine
the Nigerian traffic warden
white

the Afghan phone repair stall owner
white

the Indian corner shop owner
white

the Thai manicurist
white
imagine
if all of the workers in this city were white

the Lebanese kebab seller
white

the Syrian car washer
white

the Ghanaian road sweeper
white

imagine if all of the workers in this city were white

who would
then
be able to split us
apart
see?

imagine
why they did that

made believe
that words
said often enough
could separate us

imagine
if the colour of our blood
and the stench of our sweat
was more important
than the colour of our skin

who would
then
be able to split us
apart
see?

why
they did that?

units of damage

in memory of Errol Graham

they found a small wooden box by his bed
that you or me would've kept something nice from our past in
his 4-stone body was laid out on the floor beside it like a mat
the coroner said
it contained two back teeth and the pair of pliers
he'd used to pull them out with
cut off he turned even more in on himself
tipped his world even further up on its head
long ago he'd stopped cycling the 2-hours it took
to see his grandkids
tins of fish found in his cupboard were 4-years out of date
what a state
what a State we pay our taxes to
to look after men who can't look after themselves
while turning blind eyes to avoiders
leaving holes in the fence for them to push their cash through
then pinching pennies back off the poor

DWP pulled the cash, said his situation didn't demand an
immediate payment
the claim he'd put in wasn't relevant to his situation
of course it was fucking relevant – he was our people – a citizen
not just a unit of dough
but you deal in units of dough don't you
units of cost, units of damage
your pockets have holes we feed cash into that end up in the
stomachs of Lords
not inside Errol's stomach
but fed to your saggy-titted tousled-haired confederates
your bitches in bearskins waving about a contract
you think we don't know this
all of us seen as units of cost
units of damage

you outsource to companies who employ people that stink of
nothing but training
who've had all of their humanity trained out of them
then you put them on the phone
to script-speak to people like Errol

look at yourself...
you did this to one of us!
because of an unyielding script
because of a points system that's had its eyes taken out
because it's always just another day
of power and numbers to you

us hordes of nothing

I go to the supermarket
in my lunch break
the idiots are in there
with their blood and saliva and eyelashes
feeling melons
feeling avocados
they pick them up in their hands
press them squeeze them
like they are the breasts or testicles
of a great love

their fingers are ugly
they are the parts of hands
that have done
nothing
their hearts have done
nothing
their eyes
show nothing
they are
nothing
we are all
nothing
together

you could hang us all up on a wall on hooks
with our heads half lopped off
with our insides turned out
and they'd all feel
nothing

they all
have been exposed to nothing for so long
that nothing has become
everything
and they work work work
so that they can make nothing
happen again

they are so good at being nothing
that they have made nothing happen
almost everywhere

nothing is under their fingernails
nothing is in their eyes
nothing is on their tongues
on their skin
they stink
of it

it's got to such a stage now
that if anything ever came along
that was something again
then they would vilify it
bash it where they think it has a head
stick it with a knife where they think it has a heart
try to make it feel
as unneeded and lonely as possible
so that it could eventually feel
that it was nothing again

just like the rest of us
hordes
of nothing

motivation motivation motivation

most of the controllers walk in on death's door
slump down in their controller's chairs
and groan at the prospect of ten o'clock
which is when the various industries we service
wake up and start their day's long sluice of demands

in that hour before ten
they sometimes muster up
a bit of conversation
and they tell each other
about how mad their women are
about how the transport system gets them down
about how the price of coffee is a crime
and about how they got drunk again on cheap rose wine
watching Blade Runner into the early hours once again
before falling asleep on the couch
only to be woken up at half-past three
by one of their daughters
having a nightmare about being caught on a mudflat
and slowly being sucked out to sea

after ten
the supervisors come out
to make sure they know
that the game is on
and all of the controllers sigh a little
realising once again
that this game is not the game
they want to be a part of
but the one they have no choice but to play
if they want their daughters to at least have a roof
under which she can have her nightmares

last week of the month

it's that time again
when the lemons have been scooped and scraped down to the
skin
everything sucked clean of its proteins and fat
every shell prized open
each ear spoken to every hand shook
£600 back on a twoer loan ain't an option
just gotta keep your nose close to the ground
keep 'em peeled palms open fingers pumping with blood
primed like a chameleon's tongue
ready to snap any loose meat from the air

the automation that's going on in the supermarkets
should be a crime –
the beep beeps replacing all of those jobs – fucking criminal
but at this time of the month it helps you to slide passed the scan
the tins of tuna baked beans ham off the bone
slip a bottle of wine turned barcode away

the bus is packed so you slip on at the back
standing there with a mind lost
in the drilling and plumbing of prospecting for more –
did you turn over their leaf?
did you look in the basement of that?
what if you called them?
what could you get out of that?
but the mind snaps you back at your stop
from those useless intricate plans
that you know won't keep you afloat

reality is
two weeks of living and two of scavenging
it's one more than most
but this is the time when you realise that you're no more than a
sprinter
not built for lasting a full lap
every option a fifty-foot-high wall you can't climb
a padlock snapped shut for your daughter
a sandwich each night for your son
this is the time
when you have to stick all of that self-hatred in the freezer
stick that head of self-loathing below the water
hang a white tea-towel over your head
stick that black barrel into your mouth
try to hide
wait it out
until the sun rises up on the 1st
and everything
will be sweet again

payday desolation

after we have made the rent
stuffed enough money away in little brown envelopes
that means our family
can eat for another month
after we have had our bank accounts drained
of all the bills all the standing orders
that we have tied around our necks
after we have put the bit away for the dentist
the bit away for the kids' shoes the school uniform
after we have paid the electricity bill the car payments
the mobile phone contracts
taken care of the internet connection and council tax
and after we have chucked all of what we can stomach
into our pit of debt
we stand up
and smell
the desolation left around us
knowing that another month has just been ripped
from under our feet
hoping that no disasters will befall us
like the cooker breaking down
or the washing machine breaking down
or the boiler malfunctioning
or the car malfunctioning
or the ground opening up and swallowing us whole
because if it does
then we will have to draw from the £140 left
that we have set aside
in the sacred red envelope

sacred
because it is for her month's cakes
and my month's wine
which are often the only things that keep us sane
able to function
help us cover up
this monthly desolation of ours
spread the occasional smile
all over its ugly face

every language under the moon and the stars

I didn't want these hands
these hands that tap away at keypads all day
allocating out jobs to couriers
these hands that tare open my pay-packet every month
only to find almost all of it gone
eaten away by the rent and the bills
the standing orders and CCJ's

I didn't want these hands that pick up the phone
only to be screamed and cunted at by the people from sales
whose customers haven't had
a 'smooth experience'
these hands that the debt has put in chains
who can't even earn enough
to unpick the locks

no
I didn't want these hands
I wanted the hands of Beethoven
lifting a glass of port up to his lips after he'd finished the 5th
I wanted the hands of Jimi Hendrix
that could make a guitar speak every language under the moon
and the stars
I wanted the hands of Van Gogh
that had the guts to slice his own ear off
leaving behind only the sunflowers and stars
as remains

anything
but these hands
these whores of my body
these mere picks
that I am stuck with

I wanted a pair of
hands that I owned
that were ruled
by my guts
rather than these
needy and afraid
shovels of theirs

how we survive

the guitar that Bill plays each night
and in his makeshift band
touring the pubs and clubs of Hertfordshire every weekend
helps him get through the stresses of the day

the violin that Merve has been trying to master
every night for the last 8-years
has helped him deal with and package up all of the shit
he goes through each day
so that it can almost all
be thrown away

the paintings that Roberto paints
helps him turn out whatever it is going on inside his head
so that up there
it can almost become light and air again
rather than remaining the dingy suffocating trap
that years of 4-on 4-off night shifts
can set

the Airfix models that Andy makes every night
then hangs from the ceiling of his attic
or spreads out across its floor
trying to replicate the Battle of Midway
or the Battle of Britain
helps him clean away all of the crap
that gets thrown at him each day
so that sometimes it can feel like he is a different Andy
an Andy who doesn't only work 11-hour shifts
as a courier controller

the beer we all drink
the wine we all sip
the pills we all pop
the poems we write and the women we love
who sometimes love us back
help the rest of us
also feel like we aren't just controllers
working 11-hour shifts
without a heart or a point

I don't think we would be able to manage it
be able to keep on going back
without all of these systems
we have constructed
without all of these techniques
we have developed
just so that we were able
to survive

when you see the world almost drunk it just about works

when you see the world almost drunk
it just about works
but sober
it pulls at your teeth
hangs onto your nerves
swinging from them
and the pain is
queuing up in a busy supermarket
to buy beetroot
using a hedge trimmer
voting
brushing your teeth
kissing something alive
with a pair of tired lips

when you see the world almost drunk
it makes things
almost bearable
but sober
it is a constant
bullfight
a constant
toothache
a tiger in your mind
with its teeth in your brain
an eagle in your guts
with its talons dug in

being constantly on the edge of drunk
makes it easier
the stains
more beautiful
the wars
more winnable
the bills
less painful
but sober
nothing but pain
and the constant
ticking
of the fake smiles
the counterfeit hands
the hair the nails
the teeth the feet
the people walking
the people talking
all of those monsters
pumping away in their dead blood

when you see the world almost drunk
it is almost bearable
to pull on your socks
fasten your belt
shave
feed yourself
but sober
nothing works
nothing is alive
even the sea and the stars
seem to be a lie
with the only answer
another drink

another taste
of that freedom

friday nights at the typer

and inside
the rising and sinking of lungs
the stomach
a sea of beer and rose wine
the half-eaten corpse of an idea
bobbing about in the tide of a gin-coloured moon
a jubilation to a god
whose name now cannot be remembered
who stands back from the edge of the lips
under the dark sanctity of a tongue
bloated by the job
the mind
a lunatic thing
tiring of the ongoing experiments
made up now of the skin-cells of a clown
scooped from under the fingernails of its laughter
jokes
the camouflage of a shoulder-blade
continually wedged up against the sun
and over here
sat in the ear
the removed·mouth of a mouse
squeaking away about the scarcity of cheese
the threat of the trap
the map in the claws of a fat cat
until finally
sleep suddenly comes
like the clunk of an irreparable fault in an engine
like the dark centre of a panther
stuck in a zoo
where the catapults and springs in the depths of its hips
have suddenly become
utterly useless

the wine and the song

there was a dead fox
in the gutter
on my way to work
run over by a car
its hip broken
so that its leg
unnaturally sat
across its back
with a paw
gently resting
over one eye

sometimes
you come across something
that makes you realise
nothing is worth doing
anymore

getting up
brushing your teeth
hoovering
the lady infuriates you
the people annoy you
busses annoy you
queues annoy you
accountants dentists university deans
supervisors traffic-wardens *baristas*
mothers bent over their little miracles
pin-head teachers pin-head politicians
sunshine
the wine
and the song

sometimes
something comes along
and takes all of the fight out of you
it is like a punch in the ribs
and you can't fill up
your lungs again

horses
ironing
rent
moths
latches
toes
tigers
petrol
earwax
come

all of it
feels pointless

except the wine
and the song

religion and the great poets

the great poets talk about religion
they have holes inside them
that have been bored out by their religion
and now feel the need to fill them
with their version of it

religion begets religion
but the sun still burns
and the people keep coming
on their knees
with their best clothes on
with their hearts open
wanting to get fed by the great poets

the people love religion
and the great poets
it is the closest they ever get
to magic
it makes them feel connected
to the Universe
to their hearts

never underestimate the feeling
of feeling superior
religion
and the great poets
have created a whole community
out of it

and I am only a controller
pretending to be a poet
uneducated
bereft of the craft
drinking wine tonight
after a long week thinking about nothing but survival
with a woman in the second year of her menopause
and all of the money trees on fire

I could do with a bit of that religion
some of that great poet's magic
but I can't seem
to find any

if we killed 99% of the world's poets

the poets write such amazing sentences
they are like the arms of a tree
reaching out into the air
waving all of their little leaves about

it astonishes us
such life
such vibrancy
never endangered

in Autumn
the poets are even more astonishing
they wield their arms about
letting their leaves fall
with just the right amount of rage and courage
all over the page

in Winter
they tell us about their agony
how hard it is to build a leaf
that can move
but they manage it

and then when Summer comes around again
they are floating them out ten to the dozen
making us all feel so warm and safe

I don't know what we'd do without them
these poets
with leaves

if I had my way
I'd kill them all
press their still fresh bodies
into the earth
so the Earth could benefit
from their power
and healing
love

I don't know
I just think that killing 99% of world's poets
would be a good thing
for the planet

it needs a rest from them